Better Homes and Gardens®

EVERYDAY easy recipes

Irresistibly fresh meals in just **20 minutes!**

WILEY

John Wiley & Sons, Inc.

Meredith Corporation

Editor: Jessica Saari Christensen

Contributing Editor: Mary Williams

Recipe Development and Testing: Better Homes and Gardens Test Kitchen

John Wiley & Sons, Inc.

Publisher: Natalie Chapman

Associate Publisher: Jessica Goodman

Executive Editor: Anne Ficklen

Editor: Adam Kowit

Editorial Assistant: Cecily McAndrews

Production Director: Diana Cisek

Senior Production Editor: Jacqueline Beach

Cover Design: Suzanne Sunwoo

Design and Layout: Tai Blanche; Kim Hopkins and Mindy Samuelson, Waterbury Publications, Inc.

Manufacturing Manager: Tom Hyland

Our seal assures you that every recipe in *Everyday Easy Recipes* has been tested in the Better Homes and Gardens® Test Kitchen. This means that each recipe is practical and reliable and meets our high standards of taste appeal. We guarantee your satisfaction with this book for as long as you own it.

For general information on our other products and services or for technical support, please contact our Customer Care Department within the United States at (800) 762-2974, outside the United States at (317) 572-3993 or fax (317) 572-4002.

Wiley also publishes its books in a variety of electronic formats. Some content that appears in print may not be available in electronic books. For more information about Wiley products, visit our web site at www.wiley.com.

Library of Congress Cataloging-in-Publication Data:

Everyday easy recipes irresistibly fresh meals in just 20 minutes! / by Better homes and gardens.

p. cm.

At head of title: Better homes and gardens

Includes index.

ISBN 978-0-470-54663-5 (pbk.)

1. Quick and easy cookery. I. Better homes and gardens. II. Title: Better homes and gardens.

TX833.5.E93 2010

641.5'55--dc22

2009045473

Printed in the United States of America

10 9 8 7 6 5 4 3 2 1

Cover photo: Saucy Shrimp and Veggies, page 90

CONTENTS

Introduction

Over-booked schedules leave little room for preparing and enjoying family meals. Many days, squeezing a meal in between work, school, and recreational pursuits seems nearly impossible. Good news—even with these everyday time constraints, great tasting meals are definitely doable, and surprisingly easy.

Let Everyday Easy Recipes be your guide to fast, fresh meals every night. By using a combination of shortcut products, items from your pantry shelves, and a healthy helping of fresh fruits, vegetables, and herbs, every recipe is ready in 20 minutes or less. Better yet, these fast, easy, and delicious meals won't break the bank.

Revive dinnertime in your house with these exciting fresh recipes. Sneak a peek and see how easy mealtime can be.

PANTRY STAPLES

Of course when you have the ingredients you need on hand, these stress-free recipes are even easier to get to the table. Check out the list of staples and good-to-have items to help efficiently stock your cupboards, pantry, and refrigerator. To avoid extra shopping trips, use the helpful lists of optional foods to bring variety and spice to your meals. You'll also find a selection of quick desserts to end any meal with a sweet note.

Milk

Orange juice

Eggs

Oil (vegetable and olive)

Nonstick cooking spray

Vinegars (cider and white)

Salt, ground black pepper; black peppercorns

Garlic and garlic salt

Dried basil

Dried Italian seasoning

Chili powder

Ground cinnamon

Honey

Sugar (granulated and brown)

All-purpose flour

Mayonnaise or salad dressing

Maple syrup

Mustard

Ketchup

Soy sauce

Barbecue sauce

Cornstarch

Baking powder and soda

Butter or margarine

Corn syrup

Bread

Bottled salad dressing (Italian, ranch)

Fine dry bread crumbs (plain and seasoned)

OPTIONAL PANTRY FOODS

Dried pasta (spaghetti, angel hair, elbow macaroni, orzo, small shell macaroni)

Dried egg noodles

Panko (Japanese-style) bread crumbs

Pouches of cooked rice

Instant rice (white or brown)

Quick-cooking couscous

Ramen noodles

Pesto

Pasta sauce

Pizza sauce

Salsa

Canned tuna

Canned salmon

Canned beans (kidney, black, cannellini {white kidney})

Canned chili beans in chili gravy

Canned diced tomatoes

Stewed tomatoes (plain, Mexican-style, and Italian-style)

Canned chicken, beef, and vegetable broth

Jars of chicken and brown gravy

Unsweetened coconut milk

Nuts (almonds, pecans, walnuts, peanuts)

Orange marmalade

Currant jelly

Mango chutney

Apple juice

Fruit juice blends

Canned whole cranberry sauce

Canned pumpkin

Mandarin oranges

Flour and corn tortillas

Dried cranberries

Dried cherries

Mixed dried fruit bits

Stir-fry sauces (plum, sweet-and-sour, peanut)

Hoisin sauce

Pickles

Roasted red sweet peppers

Canned chili peppers

Chipotle peppers in adobo sauce

Balsamic vinegar

Vinaigrette salad dressing (Caesar, balsamic vinegar)

Asian-style salad dressings

Honey-Dijon salad dressing

Blue cheese salad dressing

Poppy seed salad dressing

Dried sage

Dried thyme

Curry powder

Ground cumin

Crushed red pepper

Sesame seeds

Jamaican jerk seasoning

Cajun seasoning

Lemon-pepper seasoning

Steak seasoning

Crusty bread (baguette, country Italian)

Corn muffin mix

Hoagie buns

Focaccia

Ciabatta

Pita bread rounds

Italian bread shell (Boboli)

PRODUCE TO HAVE ON HAND

Sweet peppers (green and/or red)

Carrots (whole, baby, julienne, or shredded)

Onions (yellow, red, sweet)

Green onions

Celery

Potatoes (baking, tiny new)

Sweet potatoes

Mushrooms (button, Portobello)

Cucumbers or English cucumbers

Zucchini

Yellow summer squash

Green beans

Broccoli

Cauliflower

Green cabbage

Napa cabbage

Tomatoes (including roma, cherry, and grape)

Packages of mixed salad greens

Fresh baby spinach

Shredded cabbage with carrot (coleslaw mix)

Shredded broccoli (broccoli slaw mix)

Fresh herbs (basil, oregano, flat-leaf parsley, cilantro)

Fresh ginger

Bananas

Apples

Pears

Oranges

Grapes

Kiwi fruit

Lemons and/or limes

Peeled fresh pineapple

Melons

Seasonal fruit (strawberries, blueberries, peaches, nectarines, plums)

REFRIGERATOR STANDBYS

Refrigerated pasta (fettuccine, linguine, tortellini, ravioli)

Refrigerated Alfredo pasta sauce

Refrigerated cooked polenta (plain and flavored)

Sliced cheese (cheddar, provolone, Swiss)

Shredded cheese (Parmesan, mozzarella, Monterey Jack, Italian blend, Mexican blend)

Feta cheese

Dairy sour cream

Plain yogurt

Flavored sour cream dips

Cream cheese and flavored cream cheese spreads

Refrigerated potatoes (mashed, mashed sweet, diced, and wedges)

Refrigerated biscuits and cornbread twists

Sliced bacon

Refrigerated cooked beef roast au jus

Cooked or smoked turkey breast portions

Cooked ham

Deli meats (ham, roast beef, turkey)

Cooked or grilled chicken breast strips

Roasted chicken

Smoked sausage

Cooked bratwurst

CHAPTER 1

POULTRY

CHILI CHICKEN AND PASTA

Start to Finish: 20 minutes | Makes: 4 servings

6 ounces dried angel hair pasta

3 ears fresh corn

4 small skinless, boneless chicken breast halves

1½ teaspoons chili powder

¼ teaspoon salt

¼ teaspoon freshly ground black pepper

4 tablespoons olive or vegetable oil

2 medium tomatoes, sliced

3 tablespoons lime or lemon juice

Snipped fresh flat-leaf parsley (optional)

Lime or lemon halves (optional)

1 Cook pasta in lightly salted boiling water according to package directions. Cut corn from cobs; add to pasta the last 2 minutes of cooking. Drain pasta and corn in colander; rinse with cold water until cool.

2 Meanwhile, sprinkle chicken with 1 teaspoon of the chili powder, the salt, and pepper. In a large skillet heat 1 tablespoon of the oil over medium heat. Add chicken; cook for 8 to 10 minutes or until chicken is no longer pink (170°F), turning once.

3 For dressing, in a screw-top jar combine the remaining 3 tablespoons oil, the remaining ½ teaspoon chili powder, and the lime juice; shake to combine.

4 Divide chicken, corn, tomato slices, and pasta among 4 plates. Drizzle with dressing; sprinkle lightly with additional salt and pepper. If desired, sprinkle with parsley and serve with lime halves.

Nutrition Facts per serving: 480 cal., 17 g total fat (3 g sat. fat), 66 mg chol., 232 mg sodium, 49 g carb., 4 g dietary fiber, 35 g protein. **Daily Values:** 19 % vit. A, 28 % vit. C.

CHICKEN WITH PARMESAN NOODLES

Start to Finish: 20 minutes | Makes: 4 servings

1 9-ounce package refrigerated linguine

2 tablespoons butter or margarine

4 large carrots, thinly sliced

1½ pounds skinless, boneless chicken breast halves, cut into 1-inch pieces

¼ cup purchased basil pesto

¼ cup finely shredded Parmesan cheese (1 ounce)

Fresh basil (optional)

1 Cook pasta according to package directions.

2 Meanwhile, in a very large skillet melt 1 tablespoon of the butter over medium heat. Add carrots; cook for 3 minutes. Add chicken; cook and stir for 4 to 5 minutes or until chicken is no longer pink. Add pesto; toss to coat.

3 Drain pasta; return to pan. Toss pasta with the remaining 1 tablespoon butter. Serve with chicken mixture. Sprinkle with Parmesan cheese. If desired, top with basil.

Nutrition Facts per serving: 567 cal., 19 g total fat (8 g sat. fat), 164 mg chol., 452 mg sodium, 47 g carb., 5 g dietary fiber, 52 g protein. **Daily Values:** 388 % vit. A, 11 % vit. C, 19 % calcium, 16 % iron.

SKIP-A-STEP CHICKEN RISOTTO

Start to Finish: 20 minutes | **Makes:** 4 servings

- 1 **14.8-ounce pouch cooked original long grain rice**
- 1 **5.2-ounce container semi-soft cheese with garlic and fine herbs**
- 1¾ **cups milk, plus more as needed**
- 12 **ounces asparagus spears, trimmed and cut into 2-inch pieces**
- 1 **2¼- to 2½-pound purchased roasted chicken**
- 2 **large tomatoes, coarsely chopped**
   Salt and ground black pepper
   Finely shredded Parmesan cheese (optional)

1 Heat rice according to package directions. Meanwhile, in a medium skillet heat semi-soft cheese; stir in milk. Add rice and asparagus; cook, covered, over medium heat for 7 minutes, stirring occasionally.

2 Meanwhile, remove skin and bones from chicken and discard. Coarsely chop chicken. Stir chicken and tomato into the rice mixture; cook and stir about 1 minute more or until heated through. If necessary, stir in additional milk until desired consistency. Season to taste with salt and pepper. If desired, sprinkle with Parmesan cheese.

Nutrition Facts per serving: 645 cal., 35 g total fat (15 g sat. fat), 168 mg chol., 955 mg sodium, 47 g carb., 4 g dietary fiber, 38 g protein. **Daily Values:** 29 % vit. A, 23 % vit. C, 17 % calcium, 23 % iron.

GINGERED CHICKEN AND FRIED RICE

Start to Finish: 30 minutes | **Makes:** 4 servings

- 1 **tablespoon cooking oil**
- 4 **chicken drumsticks**
- 1 **1-inch piece fresh ginger, peeled and finely chopped (2 tablespoons)**
- 2 **tablespoons soy sauce**
- 2 **large carrots, chopped or sliced**
- 1 **14.8-ounce package cooked long grain rice**
- 8 **ounces sugar snap peas**
- ½ **cup chopped red sweet pepper (optional)**
- 4 **eggs, beaten**
   Sliced green onion (optional)
   Soy sauce and/or toasted sesame oil (optional)

1 In large nonstick skillet heat oil over medium-high heat. Add chicken, half of the ginger, and soy sauce; brown chicken on all sides. Add ½ cup water; cook, covered, 15 minutes or until no pink remains in chicken (180°F).

2 In covered microwave-safe dish place carrots, remaining ginger, and 2 tablespoons water. Microwave on 100% power (high) for 4 minutes. Add rice, peas, and pepper. Microwave, covered, 5 minutes more; stir twice.

3 Remove chicken and juices from skillet. Wipe skillet with paper towels; return to heat. Add eggs; cook and stir 30 seconds to scramble. Stir in rice mixture; heat through. Serve chicken and juices with fried rice, and if desired, green onions, with soy sauce and/or sesame oil.

Nutrition Facts per serving: 421 cal., 17 g total fat (4 g sat. fat), 271 mg chol., 667 mg sodium, 42 g carb., 4 g dietary fiber, 25 g protein. **Daily Values:** 1 % vit. A, 64 % vit. C, 7 % calcium, 19 % iron.

QUICK CHICKEN PANZANELLA

Start to Finish: 20 minutes | **Makes:** 4 servings

1 **14.5-ounce can diced tomatoes with green pepper, celery, and onions, undrained**

3 **tablespoons olive oil**
Dash salt
Dash ground black pepper

1 **2- to 2¼-pound purchased roasted chicken**

4 **cups cubed Italian bread**

2 **medium cucumbers, halved lengthwise and sliced**

1 **cup torn fresh basil or spinach**

1 Spoon off 2 tablespoons of the tomato liquid and place in a small bowl. Stir in 1 tablespoon of the olive oil, the salt, and pepper; set aside. Remove skin and bones from chicken and discard. Cut chicken into pieces; set aside.

2 In a large skillet heat the remaining 2 tablespoons olive oil over medium heat. Add bread; heat and stir about 5 minutes or until golden. Transfer bread to a medium bowl. Add diced tomatoes; toss to mix. Divide bread mixture among 4 plates. Add chicken, cucumber, and basil. Pass the tomato-oil mixture.

Nutrition Facts per serving: 596 cal., 27 g total fat (6 g sat. fat), 92 mg chol., 824 mg sodium, 50 g carb., 4 g dietary fiber, 37 g protein. **Daily Values:** 21 % vit. A, 17 % vit. C, 15 % calcium, 27 % iron.

ALMOST A POT PIE

Start to Finish: 20 minutes Oven: 425°F | Makes: 4 servings

½ of a 15-ounce package rolled refrigerated unbaked pie crust (1 crust)
2 tablespoons vegetable oil
1 pound skinless, boneless chicken breast halves, cut into ½-inch pieces
1 cup thinly sliced carrot (optional)
3 tablespoons all-purpose flour
1½ cups chicken broth
2 cups fresh pea pods, halved crosswise
½ cup chopped fresh basil
Salt and ground black pepper

1 Preheat oven to 425°F. If necessary, microwave pie crust according to package directions to bring to room temperature. Unroll pie crust on a large baking sheet; cut into 8 wedges. Separate wedges slightly. Bake for 8 to 10 minutes or until golden.

2 Meanwhile, in a very large skillet heat oil over medium heat. Add chicken and, if desired, carrot; cook until chicken is brown and carrot is crisp-tender. Stir in flour. Add broth; cook and stir until thickened and bubbly. Add pea pods; cook for 1 minute. Stir in basil. Season to taste with salt and pepper.

3 Divide chicken mixture evenly among 4 shallow bowls. Serve with pie crust wedges.

Nutrition Facts per serving: 462 cal., 22 g total fat (6 g sat. fat), 72 mg chol., 782 mg sodium, 33 g carb., 1 g dietary fiber, 29 g protein. **Daily Values:** 13 % vit. A, 35 % vit. C, 4 % calcium, 10 % iron.

CHICKEN-AND-PIEROGIE TOSS

Start to Finish: 20 minutes | **Makes:** 4 servings

- 1 **12.84-ounce package frozen potato and cheese miniature pierogies**
- 12 **ounces asparagus spears, cut into 1½-inch pieces**
- 1 **tablespoon olive oil**
- 1 **pound skinless, boneless chicken breast halves, cubed**
- 1 **15-ounce can pizza sauce**
- ¾ **cup shredded mozzarella cheese**

1 Cook pierogies and asparagus in boiling lightly salted water for 5 minutes; drain.

2 Meanwhile, in a very large skillet heat olive oil over medium heat. Add chicken; cook and stir about 3 minutes or until chicken is no longer pink. Stir in pizza sauce; heat through. Add pierogies and asparagus. Sprinkle with cheese.

Nutrition Facts per serving: 428 cal., 13 g total fat (4 g sat. fat), 82 mg chol., 1034 mg sodium, 38 g carb., 3 g dietary fiber, 40 g protein. **Daily Values:** 20 % vit. A, 28 % vit. C, 20 % calcium, 25 % iron.

CHICKEN AND ASPARAGUS SKILLET SUPPER

Start to Finish: 20 minutes | **Makes:** 4 servings

- 8 **skinless, boneless chicken thighs**
  Salt and ground black pepper
- 3 **slices bacon, coarsely chopped**
- ½ **cup chicken broth**
- 1 **pound asparagus spears, trimmed**
- 1 **small yellow summer squash, halved crosswise and cut lengthwise into ½-inch strips**
- 2 **tablespoons water**
- 4 **green onions, cut into 2-inch pieces**

1 Sprinkle chicken lightly with salt and pepper. In a very large skillet cook chicken and bacon over medium-high heat for 12 minutes, turning occasionally to brown evenly. Carefully add broth; cook, covered, for 3 to 5 minutes more or until chicken is tender and no longer pink (180°F).

2 Meanwhile, in a microwave-safe 2-quart square baking dish combine asparagus, squash, and water. Sprinkle lightly with salt and pepper. Cover with vented plastic wrap. Microwave on 100% power (high) for 3 to 5 minutes or until vegetables are crisp-tender; stir once.

3 Using a slotted spoon, divide vegetables among 4 plates. Drizzle with a little of the chicken cooking liquid. Top with chicken and bacon. Sprinkle with green onion.

Nutrition Facts per serving: 320 cal., 18 g total fat (6 g sat. fat), 134 mg chol., 626 mg sodium, 5 g carb., 2 g dietary fiber, 32 g protein. **Daily Values:** 15 % vit. A, 13 % vit. C, 5 % calcium, 18 % iron.

CHICKEN WITH APRICOTS

Start to Finish: 20 minutes | **Makes:** 4 servings

1¼ cups dried orzo (about 8 ounces)

1 5-ounce can unpeeled apricot halves in light syrup

4 small skinless, boneless chicken breast halves (1 to 1¼ pounds)
   Salt and ground black pepper

1½ teaspoons curry powder

2 tablespoons olive or vegetable oil

6 green onions

1 Cook orzo according to package directions; drain. Drain apricot halves, reserving ½ cup syrup.

2 Meanwhile, sprinkle chicken with salt, pepper, and ½ teaspoon of the curry powder. In a very large skillet heat oil over medium heat. Add chicken; cook for 8 to 10 minutes or until chicken is no longer pink (170°F), turning once. Add apricots, cut sides down, the last 2 minutes of cooking. Transfer to serving plates.

3 While chicken cooks, cut green tops of 2 of the green onions into thick diagonal slices; set aside. Chop remaining green onions. Add chopped green onion and remaining 1 teaspoon curry powder to skillet; cook for 1 minute. Stir in reserved syrup and drained orzo. Spoon onto plates. Sprinkle with green onion tops.

Nutrition Facts per serving: 514 cal., 10 g total fat (2 g sat. fat), 82 mg chol., 330 mg sodium, 64 g carb., 5 g dietary fiber, 41 g protein. **Daily Values:** 34 % vit. A, 12 % vit. C, 6 % calcium, 15 % iron.

CRUSTED CHICKEN WITH MAPLE-LACED SQUASH

Start to Finish: 20 minutes | Oven: 450°F | Makes: 4 servings

Nonstick cooking spray
14 to 16 ounces chicken breast tenderloins
Salt and ground black pepper
¾ cup packaged cornflakes crumbs
3 tablespoons pure maple syrup or maple-flavored syrup
1 10- to 12-ounce package frozen cooked winter squash
¼ cup pecan pieces

1 Preheat oven to 450°F. Line a baking sheet with foil; lightly coat foil with cooking spray. Sprinkle chicken lightly with salt and pepper. Place crumbs in a shallow dish. Place 1 tablespoon of the syrup in a small bowl; brush syrup lightly on both sides of chicken. Coat chicken on both sides with cornflakes crumbs. Place chicken on prepared baking sheet. Bake for 9 to 11 minutes or until chicken is no longer pink (170°F).

2 Meanwhile, place squash in a microwave-safe 1½-quart casserole. Microwave, uncovered, on 100% power (high) for 5 to 6 minutes or until heated through; stir twice. Stir in 1 tablespoon of the syrup. Season to taste with salt and pepper.

3 In a small skillet heat pecans over medium-high heat for 2 to 3 minutes or until lightly toasted, stirring frequently. To serve, divide squash mixture and chicken among 4 plates. Drizzle with the remaining 1 tablespoon syrup; sprinkle with the toasted pecans.

Nutrition Facts per serving: 296 cal., 6 g total fat (1 g sat. fat), 58 mg chol., 333 mg sodium, 35 g carb., 2 g dietary fiber, 26 g protein. **Daily Values:** 68 % vit. A, 9 % vit. C, 5 % calcium, 25 % iron.

PINEAPPLE CHICKEN

Start to Finish: 20 minutes | Makes: 4 servings

1½ pounds skinless, boneless chicken thighs
½ teaspoon salt
½ teaspoon curry seasoning blend (optional)
2 tablespoons olive oil
1 fresh pineapple, peeled and cored
1 red sweet pepper, cut into bite-size strips
1 serrano pepper, thinly sliced (optional)
¾ cup unsweetened coconut milk
1 tablespoon packed brown sugar

1 Sprinkle chicken with salt and, if desired, curry seasoning. In a very large skillet heat 1 tablespoon of the olive oil over high heat. Add chicken; brown quickly on both sides. Reduce heat to medium-high and continue cooking about 12 minutes or until chicken is tender and no longer pink (180°F), turning occasionally to brown evenly.

2 Cut pineapple into large pieces; set aside.

3 For sauce, in a large skillet heat the remaining 1 tablespoon olive oil over medium-high heat. Add sweet pepper; cook about 3 minutes or until crisp-tender. Remove sweet pepper from skillet; set aside. Add pineapple to skillet and cook until brown, turning occasionally. If desired, add serrano pepper to pineapple; cook for 1 minute more. Stir coconut milk and brown sugar into skillet; heat through.

4 Divide chicken and pineapple among 4 shallow bowls; spoon sauce over chicken and pineapple. Top with sweet pepper strips.

Nutrition Facts per serving: 443 cal., 24 g total fat (12 g sat. fat), 141 mg chol., 448 mg sodium, 23 g carb., 3 g dietary fiber, 35 g protein. **Daily Values:** 22 % vit. A, 137 % vit. C, 4 % calcium, 17 % iron.

QUICK COCONUT CHICKEN

Start to Finish: 20 minutes | **Oven:** 450°F | **Makes:** 4 servings

¾ **cup panko (Japanese-style) breadcrumbs**

⅓ **cup shredded coconut**

½ **cup mango chutney**

2 **tablespoons butter or margarine, melted**

¼ **teaspoon salt**

¼ **teaspoon ground black pepper**

14 **to 16 ounces chicken breast tenderloins**

1 **fresh mango**

1 Preheat oven to 450°F. Line a baking sheet with foil; set aside. In a small bowl combine breadcrumbs and coconut; set aside.

2 Place chutney in another small bowl; snip any large fruit pieces. Stir in melted butter, salt, and pepper. Using tongs, dip each chicken piece into the chutney mixture. Dip in breadcrumb mixture to coat. Arrange chicken on the prepared baking sheet. Sprinkle any remaining crumb mixture over chicken.

3 Bake for 10 to 12 minutes or until coating is brown and chicken is no longer pink.

4 Meanwhile, seed, peel, and chop mango. Transfer chicken to a serving platter. Sprinkle with mango.

Nutrition Facts per serving: 339 cal., 10 g total fat (6 g sat. fat), 73 mg chol., 545 mg sodium, 35 g carb., 2 g dietary fiber, 25 g protein. **Daily Values:** 16 % vit. A, 34 % vit. C, 2 % calcium, 5 % iron.

TRIPLE MANGO CHICKEN

Start to Finish: 20 minutes | **Makes:** 4 servings

1 **tablespoon olive oil**

4 **small skinless, boneless chicken breast halves**

1 **mango, seeded, peeled, and cubed**

½ **cup mango-blend fruit drink***

¼ **cup mango chutney**

2 **medium zucchini, thinly sliced lengthwise****

¼ **cup water**

Salt

Crushed red pepper

1 In a very large skillet heat olive oil over medium-high heat; reduce heat to medium. Add chicken; cook for 6 minutes; turn. Add mango cubes, mango drink, and mango chutney; cook for 4 to 6 minutes more or until chicken is no longer pink (170°F), stirring occasionally.

2 Meanwhile, in a microwave-safe 2-quart square dish place zucchini and the water. Cover with vented plastic wrap. Microwave on 100% power (high) for 2 to 3 minutes; stir once; drain. Divide zucchini among 4 plates. Place chicken on top of zucchini. Season to taste with salt and crushed red pepper.

Nutrition Facts per serving: 274 cal., 9 g total fat (1 g sat. fat), 66 mg chol., 277 mg sodium, 22 g carb., 2 g dietary fiber, 28 g protein. **Daily Values:** 16 % vit. A, 59 % vit. C, 4 % calcium, 8 % iron.

*TIP: Mango nectar, carrot juice, or orange juice may be substituted for the mango-blend fruit drink.

**TIP: A vegetable peeler helps to quickly slice the zucchini lengthwise.

CHICKEN-PINEAPPLE FAJITAS

Start to Finish: 20 minutes | Oven: 350°F | Makes: 4 servings (2 fajitas each)

- 8 6-inch flour tortillas
  Nonstick cooking spray
- 4 1-inch slices peeled fresh pineapple (½ to ⅔ of a pineapple)
- 1 pound skinless, boneless chicken breast halves
- 2 small red and/or orange sweet peppers, cut into thin bite-size strips
- 2 teaspoons Jamaican jerk seasoning
- ⅛ teaspoon ground black pepper
- 1 tablespoon vegetable oil
  Fresh cilantro (optional)
  Lime wedges (optional)

1 Preheat oven to 350°F. Wrap tortillas in foil. Place foil packet in the oven. Meanwhile, lightly coat a very large nonstick skillet with cooking spray; heat over medium-high heat. Add pineapple slices; cook for 4 to 6 minutes or until light brown, turning once. Transfer pineapple to a cutting board; set aside.

2 Meanwhile, cut chicken into thin strips. In a large bowl toss chicken and sweet pepper with jerk seasoning and black pepper.

3 In the same skillet heat oil over medium-high heat. Add chicken mixture; cook and stir for 4 to 6 minutes or until chicken is no longer pink. Meanwhile, core and coarsely chop pineapple slices. Divide pineapple and chicken mixture among the warm tortillas. If desired, serve with cilantro and lime.

Nutrition Facts per serving: 393 cal., 10 g total fat (2 g sat. fat), 66 mg chol., 633 mg sodium, 43 g carb., 4 g dietary fiber, 32 g protein. **Daily Values:** 26 % vit. A, 122 % vit. C, 11 % calcium, 18 % iron.

SESAME AND GINGER CHICKEN

Start to Finish: 20 minutes | **Makes:** 4 servings

1 **pound skinless, boneless chicken breast halves, cut into bite-size pieces**
  Salt and ground black pepper
  Nonstick cooking spray
¼ **cup bottled light Asian-style salad dressing with sesame and ginger**
2 **cups packaged julienne or shredded fresh carrot**
⅛ **teaspoon crushed red pepper**
1 **head Boston or Bibb lettuce, separated into leaves**
¼ **cup honey-roasted peanuts, chopped**
  Lime wedges (optional)

1 Sprinkle chicken lightly with salt and black pepper. Lightly coat a large skillet with cooking spray; heat over medium-high heat. Add chicken; cook and stir for 3 minutes or until brown. Add 1 tablespoon of the dressing and the carrot to skillet; cook and stir for 2 to 3 minutes more or until carrot is crisp-tender and chicken is no longer pink. Stir in crushed red pepper.

2 On a large platter or 4 plates arrange 4 stacks of lettuce leaves. Fill lettuce stacks with chicken mixture. Sprinkle with peanuts. Serve with remaining dressing and, if desired, lime wedges.

Nutrition Facts per serving: 231 cal., 7 g total fat (1 g sat. fat), 66 mg chol., 436 mg sodium, 12 g carb., 3 g dietary fiber, 29 g protein. **Daily Values:** 212 % vit. A, 10 % vit. C, 5 % calcium, 9 % iron.

CHIMICHURRI CHICKEN

Start to Finish: 20 minutes | Makes: 4 servings

- 4 **skinless, boneless chicken breast halves**
- 3 **tablespoons vegetable oil**
- ½ **teaspoon salt**
- ¼ **teaspoon ground black pepper**
- 1 **ounce fresh young green beans**
- 1 **tablespoon water**
- ¾ **cup packed fresh flat-leaf parsley**
- 1 **tablespoon cider vinegar**
- 2 **cloves garlic, halved**
- ¼ **teaspoon crushed red pepper**
- 1 **lemon**

1 Brush chicken with 1 tablespoon of the oil. Sprinkle chicken with ¼ teaspoon of the salt and the black pepper. For a charcoal grill, grill chicken on the rack of uncovered grill directly over medium coals for 12 to 15 minutes or until no longer pink (170°F), turning once halfway through grilling. (For a gas grill preheat grill. Reduce heat to medium. Place chicken on rack over heat. Cover; grill as above.)

2 Place beans in a microwave-safe 1½-quart dish. Add the water. Cover with vented plastic wrap. Microwave on 100% power (high) for 3 minutes; drain.

3 For chimichurri sauce, in a small food processor combine parsley, the remaining 2 tablespoons oil, the vinegar, garlic, the remaining ¼ teaspoon salt, and the crushed red pepper; process until nearly smooth. Finely shred peel from the lemon and cut lemon in half. Serve chicken and green beans topped with chimichurri sauce and lemon peel. Squeeze lemon juice over all.

Nutrition Facts per serving: 281 cal., 12 g total fat (2 g sat. fat), 82 mg chol., 376 mg sodium, 8 g carb., 3 g dietary fiber, 35 g protein. **Daily Values:** 32 % vit. A, 57 % vit. C, 7 % calcium, 14 % iron.

TURKEY AU GRATIN

Start to Finish: 18 minutes | Makes: 4 servings

½ cup water

2½ cups packaged fresh broccoli florets, large florets cut in half

¾ cup frozen whole kernel corn

1 8-ounce tub cream cheese spread with garden vegetables

2 cups cubed cooked turkey (10 ounces)

⅓ to ½ cup milk
Salt and ground black pepper

3 ounces whole wheat crackers, crushed (about ¾ cup)

2 tablespoons butter or margarine, melted

1 In a large saucepan bring water to boiling. Add broccoli and corn; return to boiling; reduce heat. Simmer, covered, for 4 minutes. Reduce heat to low. Add cream cheese by spoonfuls, stirring gently until melted before adding more. Stir in turkey. Add enough milk to make desired consistency; heat through. Season to taste with salt and pepper.

2 To serve, divide mixture among 4 individual dishes. In a small bowl combine crushed crackers and butter; sprinkle over each serving.

Nutrition Facts per serving: 522 cal., 32 g total fat (19 g sat. fat), 125 mg chol., 651 mg sodium, 29 g carb., 4 g dietary fiber, 27 g protein. **Daily Values:** 27 % vit. A, 88 % vit. C, 16 % calcium, 14 % iron.

TURKEY AND POTATOES IN PAPRIKA SAUCE

Start to Finish: 20 minutes | Makes: 4 servings

1 pound tiny new potatoes, halved

1 medium onion, cut into thin wedges

2 tablespoons water

1 teaspoon smoked paprika or paprika

½ teaspoon salt

¼ teaspoon ground black pepper

1 tablespoon vegetable oil

1 pound turkey breast tenderloin, cut into ¾-inch cubes
Salt and ground black pepper

½ cup light dairy sour cream
Milk
Grated Parmesan cheese (optional)

1 In a 2-quart microwave-safe casserole combine potato halves, onion, the water, paprika, the ½ teaspoon salt, and the ¼ teaspoon pepper. Microwave, covered, on 100% power (high) for 8 to 10 minutes or until potato halves are tender; stir once.

2 Meanwhile, in a large skillet heat oil over medium-high heat. Sprinkle turkey lightly with salt and pepper. Cook turkey in hot oil for 4 to 6 minutes or until no longer pink, stirring occasionally.

3 Add turkey and sour cream to potato mixture. If necessary, stir in enough milk to make desired consistency. Microwave, covered, on 50% power (medium) for 1 to 2 minutes or just until heated through (do not boil). If desired, sprinkle with Parmesan cheese.

Nutrition Facts per serving: 281 cal., 7 g total fat (2 g sat. fat), 79 mg chol., 517 mg sodium, 23 g carb., 3 g dietary fiber, 31 g protein. **Daily Values:** 7 % vit. A, 21 % vit. C, 6 % calcium, 13 % iron.

TIP: For an even quicker preparation, use 1 pound deli-roasted turkey breast. Prepare as above, except omit step 2. Cut turkey into cubes and add with the sour cream to heat through.

PARMESAN-CRUSTED TURKEY WITH MASHED CAULIFLOWER

Start to Finish: 20 minutes | **Makes:** 4 servings

- 3 cups coarsely chopped cauliflower (½ of a head)
- ¼ cup water
- 2 8-ounce turkey breast tenderloins, halved horizontally
  Salt and ground black pepper
- ⅓ cup light mayonnaise or mayonnaise
- ⅓ cup finely shredded Parmesan cheese
- 3 tablespoons fine dry breadcrumbs
- 2 tablespoons butter or margarine
  Chopped fresh flat-leaf parsley and/or paprika (optional)

1 Preheat broiler. In a microwave-safe 1½-quart casserole combine cauliflower and the water. Microwave, covered, on 100% power (high) for 12 to 15 minutes or until very tender; stir once.

2 Meanwhile, sprinkle turkey lightly with salt and pepper. Place on an unheated rack of a broiler pan. Broil 4 inches from heat for 5 minutes. Turn turkey; broil 4 minutes more. Meanwhile, in a small bowl stir together mayonnaise, ¼ cup of the Parmesan cheese, and the breadcrumbs. Spread over turkey. Broil for 2 to 3 minutes more or until topping is golden and turkey is no longer pink (170°F). Add butter and the remaining Parmesan cheese to cauliflower; mash until smooth. Serve mashed cauliflower with turkey. If desired, sprinkle with parsley and/or paprika.

Nutrition Facts per serving: 310 cal., 15 g total fat (6 g sat. fat), 97 mg chol., 574 mg sodium, 10 g carb., 2 g dietary fiber, 33 g protein. **Daily Values:** 5 % vit. A, 58 % vit. C, 12 % calcium, 11 % iron.

CURRY-AND-MACADAMIA-CRUSTED TURKEY

Start to Finish: 20 minutes | **Makes:** 4 servings

½ cup mango chutney
1 teaspoon curry powder
½ teaspoon salt
¼ teaspoon ground black pepper
1½ cups water
1 cup quick-cooking couscous
2 8-ounce turkey breast tenderloins, halved horizontally
½ cup finely chopped macadamia nuts*
2 tablespoons olive or vegetable oil

1 Place chutney in a small bowl; snip any large fruit pieces. Stir in curry powder, salt, and pepper. Place half of the chutney mixture in a medium saucepan. Add the 1½ cups water. Bring to boiling. Stir in couscous. Remove from heat; cover and let stand.

2 Meanwhile, coat turkey with the remaining chutney mixture. Dip 1 side of each piece into chopped nuts.

3 In a very large skillet heat oil over medium heat. Add turkey, nut sides down; cook for 6 minutes. Turn turkey over; cook for 6 to 9 minutes more or until no pink remains (170°F). Spoon any coating remaining in pan onto turkey. Fluff couscous mixture; serve with turkey.

Nutrition Facts per serving: 796 cal., 21 g total fat (3 g sat. fat), 105 mg chol., 624 mg sodium, 92 g carb., 6 g dietary fiber, 55 g protein. **Daily Values:** 4 % vit. A, 8 % vit. C, 6 % calcium, 21 % iron.

*TIP: To quickly chop the nuts, place in a food processor; cover and process with several on/off turns until finely chopped.

CAJUN TURKEY AND MELON

Start to Finish: 18 minutes | **Makes:** 4 servings

2 8-ounce turkey breast tenderloins, halved horizontally
1 tablespoon olive oil
1½ teaspoons Cajun seasoning
6 cups torn mixed greens
1½ cups sliced cantaloupe
1 cup fresh blueberries
Crumbled farmer cheese (optional)
Bottled salad dressing of your choice

1 Brush turkey with olive oil. Sprinkle with Cajun seasoning. For a charcoal grill, grill turkey on the rack of an uncovered grill directly over medium coals for 12 to 15 minutes or until turkey is no longer pink (170°F), turning once halfway through grilling. (For a gas grill, preheat grill. Reduce heat to medium. Place turkey on grill rack over heat. Cover; grill as above.)

2 Slice turkey. Arrange greens on a serving platter. Add turkey, cantaloupe, and blueberries. If desired, top with cheese. Pass dressing.

Nutrition Facts per serving: 359 cal., 22 g total fat (4 g sat. fat), 68 mg chol., 161 mg sodium, 14 g carb., 3 g dietary fiber, 29 g protein. **Daily Values:** 56 % vit. A, 52 % vit. C, 6 % calcium, 12 % iron.

CREAMED TURKEY AND BISCUITS

Start to Finish: 20 minutes | Makes: 4 servings

4 refrigerated biscuits
1 8-ounce tub cream cheese spread with chive and onion
¾ cup milk
2½ cups coarsely shredded cooked turkey or chicken
1 6-ounce package fresh baby spinach (6 cups)
Salt and ground black pepper
½ cup whole cranberry sauce

1 Prepare biscuits according to package directions.

2 Meanwhile, in a 4-quart Dutch oven heat cream cheese over medium-low heat to soften. Whisk in milk until nearly smooth. Add turkey; heat through. Stir in spinach until coated and slightly wilted. Season to taste with salt and pepper.

3 Carefully split warm biscuits; place biscuit bottoms on plates. Spoon turkey mixture onto biscuit bottoms. Top with cranberry sauce; add biscuit tops. Serve immediately.

Nutrition Facts per serving: 530 cal., 28 g total fat (16 g sat. fat), 125 mg chol., 808 mg sodium, 33 g carb., 2 g dietary fiber, 32 g protein. **Daily Values:** 96 % vit. A, 21 % vit. C, 21 % calcium, 20 % iron.

CRANBERRY-SAUCED SAUSAGE ON SQUASH

Start to Finish: 20 minutes | Makes: 4 servings

1 large acorn squash, halved and seeded
2 tablespoons water
1 tablespoon vegetable oil
1 pound smoked turkey sausage, cut into ½-inch slices
1 medium onion, cut into thin wedges
2 medium carrots, thinly sliced
1 16-ounce can whole cranberry sauce

1 Place squash halves, cut sides down, in a baking dish; add the water. Cover with vented plastic wrap. Microwave on 100% power (high) for 7 to 10 minutes or until tender, turning the dish once for even cooking.

2 Meanwhile, in a very large skillet heat oil over medium heat. Add sausage, onion, and carrot; cook about 5 minutes or until sausage is light brown, stirring occasionally. Add cranberry sauce. Bring to boiling; reduce heat. Simmer, covered, about 5 minutes or just until carrot is tender.

3 Carefully cut squash into quarters; divide among 4 plates. Top with sausage mixture.

Nutrition Facts per serving: 447 cal., 13 g total fat (3 g sat. fat), 76 mg chol., 1038 mg sodium, 63 g carb., 5 g dietary fiber, 19 g protein. **Daily Values:** 110 % vit. A, 26 % vit. C, 6 % calcium, 13 % iron.

CHAPTER 2

MEAT

BALSAMIC-GLAZED FLANK STEAK WITH FALL FRUIT SALSA

Start to Finish: 20 minutes | Makes: 4 servings

1 pound beef flank steak
Salt and ground black pepper
3 tablespoons balsamic vinegar
2 medium red and/or green apples
1 medium pear
¼ cup dried cranberries
2 teaspoons sugar
¼ teaspoon ground cinnamon

1 Preheat broiler. Trim fat from steak. Score both sides of steak in a diamond pattern, making shallow diagonal cuts at 1-inch intervals. Sprinkle both sides lightly with salt and pepper. Place steak on unheated rack of broiler pan. Broil 3 to 4 inches from heat for 14 minutes, turning once. Brush both sides of steak with 1 tablespoon of the balsamic vinegar; broil 1 to 2 minutes more for medium (160°F).

2 Meanwhile, for fruit salsa, core and chop apples and pear. In a medium bowl combine apples, pear, cranberries, the remaining 2 tablespoons balsamic vinegar, the sugar, and cinnamon.

3 Thinly slice steak and serve with fruit salsa.

Nutrition Facts per serving: 288 cal., 9 g total fat (4 g sat. fat), 53 mg chol., 221 mg sodium, 26 g carb., 3 g dietary fiber, 27 g protein. **Daily Values:** 1 % vit. A, 8 % vit. C, 2 % calcium, 13 % iron.

CHIPOTLE STEAK

Start to Finish: 20 minutes | Makes: 4 servings

2 6- to 8-ounce beef shoulder petite tenders or beef rib-eye steaks
Salt and ground black pepper
1 canned chipotle pepper in adobo sauce, finely chopped, plus 2 teaspoons adobo sauce
¼ cup olive oil
¼ cup vinegar
3 medium tomatoes, cut into thick slices
2 medium avocados, halved, pitted, peeled, and sliced
½ of a small red onion, very thinly sliced

1 Sprinkle steaks lightly with salt and black pepper. Spread each steak with 1 teaspoon of the adobo sauce.

2 For a charcoal grill, grill steaks on the rack of an uncovered grill directly over medium coals until desired doneness, turning once. Allow 10 to 12 minutes for medium-rare (145°F) or 12 to 15 minutes for medium (160°F). (For a gas grill, preheat grill. Reduce heat to medium. Place steaks on grill rack over heat. Cover; grill as above.)

3 Meanwhile, for dressing, in a screw-top jar combine the chopped chipotle pepper, olive oil, and vinegar. Cover and shake to combine.

4 Slice steaks and arrange on 4 serving plates with tomato and avocado slices. Top with onion slices and drizzle with dressing.

Nutrition Facts per serving: 421 cal., 33 g total fat (6 g sat. fat), 50 mg chol., 221 mg sodium, 13 g carb., 7 g dietary fiber, 20 g protein. **Daily Values:** 19 % vit. A, 34 % vit. C, 3% calcium, 15 % iron.

TIP: For a creamy dressing, omit oil and vinegar and stir the chipotle pepper into ½ cup bottled ranch dressing.

CHIPOTLE STEAK

HERBED STEAKS WITH HORSERADISH

Start to Finish: 20 minutes | **Makes:** 4 servings

2 12- to 14-ounce beef top loin
steaks, 1 inch thick
Salt and ground black
pepper
2 tablespoons prepared
horseradish
1 tablespoon Dijon-style
mustard
2 teaspoons snipped fresh
flat-leaf parsley
1 teaspoon snipped fresh
thyme
Broiled cherry tomatoes
(optional)
Broiled yellow or green
sweet pepper strips
(optional)
Herbed mayonnaise
(optional)

1 Preheat broiler. Sprinkle steaks lightly with salt and pepper. Place steaks on unheated rack of broiler pan. Broil 4 inches from heat for 7 minutes.

2 Meanwhile, in a small bowl combine horseradish, mustard, parsley, and thyme. Turn steaks; broil for 8 to 9 minutes more for medium (160°F). The last 1 minute of broiling, spread with horseradish mixture. If desired, serve with broiled cherry tomatoes and sweet pepper strips, and herbed mayonnaise.

Nutrition Facts per serving: 284 cal., 15 g total fat (6 g sat. fat), 84 mg chol., 351 mg sodium, 1 g carb., 0 g dietary fiber, 33 g protein. **Daily Values:** 1 % vit. A, 5 % vit. C, 3 % calcium, 19 % iron.

TIP: Steaks may also be grilled directly over medium coals for the same amount of time.
TIP: For herbed mayonnaise, stir some prepared horseradish, Dijon-style mustard, and snipped fresh thyme or parsley into mayonnaise.

STEAK WITH SWEET POTATO–MANGO CHUTNEY

Start to Finish: 20 minutes | **Makes:** 4 servings

1 large sweet potato, peeled and diced (12 ounces)

4 6-ounce boneless beef eye round steaks, about ¾ inch thick

Salt

Steak seasoning

⅓ cup mango chutney

¼ cup dried cranberries

Fresh rosemary (optional)

1 In a medium saucepan cook sweet potato, covered, in boiling lightly salted water for 8 to 10 minutes or until tender; drain and keep warm.

2 Meanwhile, preheat a large nonstick skillet over medium-high heat. Sprinkle steaks lightly with salt and steak seasoning. Add steaks to skillet; reduce heat to medium. Cook for 8 to 10 minutes or until desired doneness. If steaks brown too quickly, reduce heat to medium-low. Transfer steaks to serving plates; cover to keep warm.

3 For sweet potato–mango chutney, add sweet potato to skillet; cook and stir about 2 minutes. Add mango chutney and cranberries to skillet. Stir gently to heat through. Season to taste with salt and steak seasoning. Serve sweet potato–mango chutney with steaks. If desired, garnish with fresh rosemary.

Nutrition Facts per serving: 344 cal., 5 g total fat (2 g sat. fat), 70 mg chol., 418 mg sodium, 32 g carb., 4 g dietary fiber, 40 g protein. **Daily Values:** 330 % vit. A, 34 % vit. C, 8 % calcium, 23 % iron.

SPICY BEEF NOODLE BOWL

Start to Finish: 20 minutes | Makes: 4 servings

- 1 tablespoon vegetable oil
- 1 pound boneless beef sirloin steak, cut into thin strips
- 2 14-ounce cans reduced-sodium beef broth
- ⅓ cup bottled peanut sauce
- 1½ cups medium egg noodles (3 ounces)
- 2 cups broccoli florets
- ¼ cup bias-sliced green onions (optional)

1 In a Dutch oven heat oil over medium-high heat. Add beef strips; cook until brown.

2 Add beef broth and peanut sauce; bring to boiling. Stir in noodles; reduce heat. Simmer, uncovered, about 4 minutes, stirring occasionally. Add broccoli; return mixture to boiling. Reduce heat; simmer, uncovered, for 3 to 4 minutes more or just until noodles are tender, stirring occasionally.

3 Divide beef and noodle mixture among 4 bowls. If desired, sprinkle with green onion.

Nutrition Facts per serving: 316 cal., 12 g total fat (3 g sat. fat), 60 mg chol., 762 mg sodium, 18 g carb., 2 g dietary fiber, 31 g protein. **Daily Values:** 6 % vit. A, 68 % vit. C, 5 % calcium, 15 % iron.

HERB-GARLIC BEEF ROAST

Start to Finish: 19 minutes | Makes: 4 servings

- 1 17-ounce package refrigerated cooked beef roast au jus
- 1 pound small round red potatoes
- 3 medium carrots
- 1 tablespoon vegetable oil
  Ground black pepper
- 3 tablespoons chopped fresh flat-leaf parsley
- 3 to 6 cloves garlic, minced
- 1 tablespoon finely shredded lemon peel

1 Place roast in a large skillet; cook, covered, over medium heat for 10 minutes. Uncover, and simmer about 5 minutes or until juices are slightly reduced.

2 Meanwhile, quarter potatoes. Peel and diagonally slice carrots into ¾-inch pieces. Place potato and carrot in a microwave-safe dish. Drizzle with oil and sprinkle with pepper; toss to coat. Tightly cover with lid or plastic wrap. Microwave on high (100% power) about 10 minutes or until tender.

3 In a small bowl combine parsley, garlic, and lemon peel.

4 To serve, stir cooked vegetables into skillet with beef and juices. Divide among 4 serving dishes. Sprinkle with herb-garlic mixture.

Nutrition Facts per serving: 311 cal., 12 g total fat (5 g sat. fat), 64 mg chol., 465 mg sodium, 28 g carb., 4 g dietary fiber, 25 g protein. **Daily Values:** 159 % vit. A, 52 % vit. C, 4 % calcium, 18 % iron.

ASIAN-GLAZED PORK

Start to Finish: 20 minutes | **Makes:** 4 servings

- 4 ounces dried angel hair pasta
- 4 boneless pork loin chops, ¾ inch thick
  Salt and ground black pepper
- 4 tablespoons orange marmalade
- 2 cups packaged shredded broccoli (broccoli slaw mix)
- 2 tablespoons bottled teriyaki sauce

1 Cook pasta according to package directions.

2 Preheat broiler. Place chops on the unheated rack of a broiler pan. Sprinkle chops lightly with salt and pepper. Broil 3 to 4 inches from heat for 5 minutes. Turn chops; broil for 4 to 6 minutes more or until done (160°F). Brush with 2 tablespoons of the marmalade the last 3 to 4 minutes of broiling.

3 Meanwhile, drain pasta. Toss hot pasta with shredded broccoli, teriyaki sauce, and the remaining 2 tablespoons marmalade. Divide pasta mixture evenly among 4 plates; top each with a chop.

Nutrition Facts per serving: 353 cal., 10 g total fat (3 g sat. fat), 73 mg chol., 592 mg sodium, 38 g carb., 2 g dietary fiber, 27 g protein. **Daily Values:** 25 % vit. A, 63 % vit. C, 6 % calcium, 15 % iron.

JAMAICAN PORK STIR-FRY

Start to Finish: 20 minutes | **Makes:** 4 servings

- 1 tablespoon vegetable oil, plus more as needed
- 1 16-ounce package frozen peppers (yellow, green, and red) and onion stir-fry vegetables
- 12 ounces pork strips for stir-frying
- 2 to 3 teaspoons Jamaican jerk seasoning
- ½ cup bottled plum sauce
  Soy sauce (optional)
  Peanuts (optional)
- 2 cups hot cooked rice or pasta

1 In a wok or large skillet heat oil over medium-high heat. Add frozen vegetables; cook and stir for 5 to 7 minutes or until vegetables are crisp-tender. Remove vegetables from wok.

2 Toss pork with jerk seasoning; add to wok. Add more oil if needed; cook and stir for 2 to 5 minutes or until pork is no longer pink.

3 Add plum sauce; stir in vegetables. Gently toss to coat; heat through. If desired, season with soy sauce and sprinkle with peanuts. Serve over hot cooked rice.

Nutrition Facts per serving: 357 cal., 9 g total fat (2 g sat. fat), 54 mg chol., 405 mg sodium, 45 g carb., 2 g dietary fiber, 22 g protein. **Daily Values:** 14 % vit. A, 68 % vit. C, 2 % calcium, 15 % iron.

TIP: If your supermarket doesn't sell pork strips, cut your own from pork loin.

JAMAICAN PORK STIR-FRY

SWEET-AND-SOUR PORK LO MEIN

Start to Finish: 18 minutes | **Makes:** 4 servings

 1 9-ounce package refrigerated linguine
 2 tablespoons vegetable oil
1½ cups packaged julienne or shredded fresh carrot
 1 large onion, cut into thin wedges
12 ounces boneless pork loin, cut into thin strips
⅓ cup orange marmalade
¼ cup cider vinegar
   Salt and ground black pepper
   Chopped peanuts (optional)

1 If desired, snip linguine into 2- to 3-inch lengths. Cook linguini according to package directions; drain.

2 Meanwhile, in a large skillet heat 1 tablespoon of the oil over medium-high heat. Add carrot and onion; cook and stir about 4 minutes or just until onion is tender. Remove vegetables from skillet. Add the remaining 1 tablespoon oil and pork to skillet; cook and stir for 3 to 4 minutes or until pork is no longer pink. Return vegetables to skillet. Add drained pasta, marmalade, and vinegar; toss to mix; heat through. Season to taste with salt and pepper. If desired, sprinkle with chopped peanuts.

Nutrition Facts per serving: 452 cal., 12 g total fat (3 g sat. fat), 121 mg chol., 252 mg sodium, 60 g carb., 4 g dietary fiber, 27 g protein. **Daily Values:** 154 % vit. A, 13 % vit. C, 6 % calcium, 13 % iron.

PEPPERY PORK CHOPS AND POTATOES

Start to Finish: 20 minutes | **Makes:** 4 servings

- 4 bone-in pork chops, ½ inch thick (about 1¼ pounds)
- 1 teaspoon Montreal steak seasoning
- 1 tablespoon vegetable oil
- 1 12-ounce jar chicken gravy
- 2 cups frozen diced hash brown potatoes with onions and peppers
- 1 8-ounce package fresh green and wax beans (about 2½ cups)

1 Sprinkle chops with steak seasoning. In a very large skillet heat oil over medium-high heat. Add chops; brown for 2 minutes on each side. Remove chops from skillet; set aside.

2 Add gravy, hash brown potatoes, and beans to the skillet. Bring to boiling; reduce heat. Simmer, covered, for 8 to 10 minutes or until beans are crisp-tender, stirring occasionally. Place chops in skillet on top of bean mixture; cook, covered, about 5 minutes or until chops are no longer pink and beans are tender.

Nutrition Facts per serving: 291 cal., 15 g total fat (4 g sat. fat), 51 mg chol., 925 mg sodium, 21 g carb., 3 g dietary fiber, 19 g protein. **Daily Values:** 4 % vit. A, 18 % vit. C, 5 % calcium, 10 % iron.

CORNMEAL-CRUSTED PORK

Start to Finish: 20 minutes | **Makes:** 4 servings

- ½ cup yellow cornmeal
- ½ teaspoon salt
- ½ teaspoon ground black pepper
- 1 egg, lightly beaten
- 1 tablespoon water
- 1 pound pork tenderloin, cut into ½-inch slices
- 2 tablespoons olive or vegetable oil
- 12 ounces fresh green beans
- 2 medium zucchini and/or yellow summer squash, thinly bias-sliced
- 2 tablespoons fresh small oregano leaves (optional)

1 In a shallow dish combine cornmeal, salt, and pepper. In another shallow dish combine egg and the water. Dip pork into egg mixture and then into cornmeal mixture to coat.

2 In a very large skillet heat oil over medium-high heat. Add pork; cook about 2 minutes per side or until no pink remains. Arrange pork on serving platter; keep warm.

3 Add green beans and zucchini to skillet; cook and stir for 6 to 8 minutes or until crisp-tender. Season to taste with salt and pepper; toss. Serve vegetables with pork. If desired, sprinkle with oregano.

Nutrition Facts per serving: 310 cal., 13 g total fat (3 g sat. fat), 127 mg chol., 385 mg sodium, 21 g carb., 5 g dietary fiber, 29 g protein. **Daily Values:** 17 % vit. A, 52 % vit. C, 6 % calcium, 19 % iron.

CORNMEAL-CRUSTED PORK

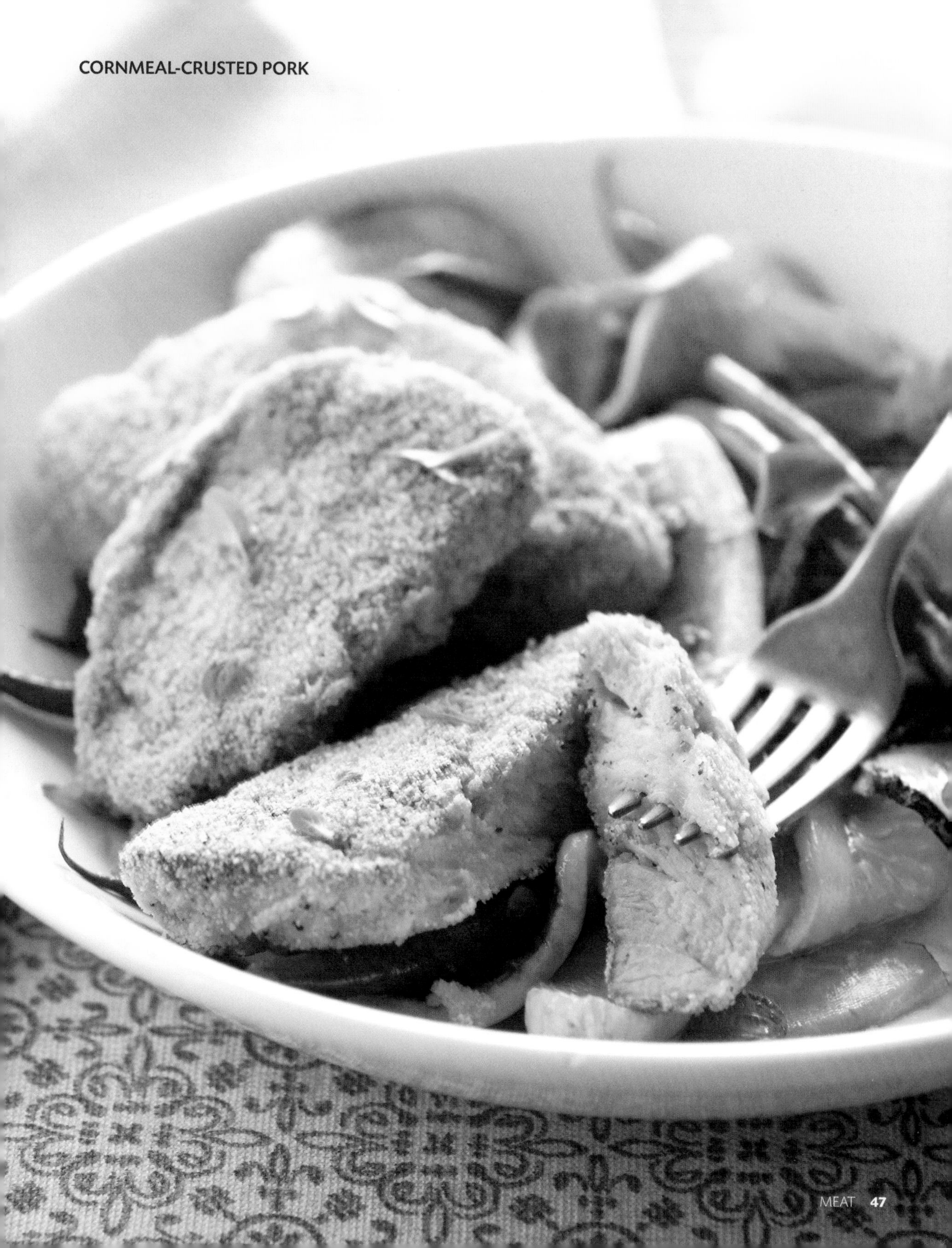

PORK AND POTATOES WITH TOMATO RELISH

Start to Finish: 20 minutes | Makes: 4 servings

1 24-ounce package refrigerated mashed potatoes

4 boneless pork loin chops, ¾ inch thick

Salt and ground black pepper

2 tablespoons olive or vegetable oil

1 large red onion, quartered and sliced (2 cups)

2 medium tomatoes, cut into thin wedges

¼ cup bottled red wine vinaigrette salad dressing

1 Prepare mashed potatoes according to microwave package directions.

2 Meanwhile, sprinkle chops lightly with salt and pepper. In a very large skillet heat oil over medium-high heat. Add chops; cook about 3 minutes. Turn chops; add onion to skillet. Cook about 10 minutes more or until chops are done (160°F), turning chops to brown evenly and stirring onion occasionally. Remove chops to 4 serving plates.

3 For tomato relish, add tomato and salad dressing to skillet; cook and stir about 1 minute more.

4 Serve chops with mashed potatoes and tomato relish. Season with additional pepper.

Nutrition Facts per serving: 433 cal., 20 g total fat (3 g sat. fat), 62 mg chol., 624 mg sodium, 32 g carb., 3 g dietary fiber, 31 g protein. **Daily Values:** 10 % vit. A, 68 % vit. C, 6 % calcium, 11 % iron.

PORK CHOPS PRIMAVERA

Start to Finish: 18 minutes | Makes: 4 servings

4 slices peppered bacon, cut into 1-inch pieces

1 12-ounce package trimmed fresh young green beans

2 tablespoons water

4 pork chops, ½ inch thick

1 tablespoon soy sauce

⅓ cup apple butter

¼ cup water

1 cup red and/or yellow cherry or grape tomatoes

1 In a very large skillet cook bacon over medium-high heat until crisp; remove with slotted spoon. Reserve 1 tablespoon drippings in the skillet. Drain bacon on paper towels; crumble bacon.

2 Meanwhile, place green beans in a 2-quart microwave-safe dish. Add the 2 tablespoons water. Microwave, covered, on 100% (high) power for 4 minutes; stir once. Drain beans; set aside.

3 Brush chops with soy sauce; add chops to drippings in skillet. Brown on both sides; add apple butter and the ¼ cup water. Reduce heat; simmer, covered, about 5 minutes. Add green beans, tomatoes, and bacon; cook, uncovered, for 3 to 5 minutes more or until tomatoes soften and sauce is thickened.

Nutrition Facts per serving: 402 cal., 16 g total fat (5 g sat. fat), 80 mg chol., 534 mg sodium, 39 g carb., 5 g dietary fiber, 27 g protein. **Daily Values:** 20 % vit. A, 35 % vit. C, 7 % calcium, 14 % iron.

APPLE-SAUCED PORK

Start to Finish: 20 minutes | Makes: 4 servings

1 pound pork tenderloin
2 tablespoons vegetable oil
2 leeks, thinly sliced
2 medium apples, cored and sliced crosswise into rings
¼ cup apple juice
⅓ cup currant jelly
2 tablespoons cider vinegar

1 Cut pork tenderloin into ½-inch slices; flatten with hand to about ¼ inch thick. In a very large skillet heat oil over medium-high heat. Add pork slices; cook about 2 minutes. Turn pork; add leeks to skillet. Cook about 2 minutes more.

2 Add apples and apple juice to skillet. Reduce heat to medium-low; simmer, covered, about 4 minutes. Using a slotted spatula, transfer pork and apples to a serving platter; keep warm.

3 For sauce, stir currant jelly and vinegar into juices in skillet. Bring to boiling. Boil gently, uncovered, about 2 minutes or until slightly thickened. Spoon sauce over pork and apples.

Nutrition Facts per serving: 327 cal., 9 g total fat (2 g sat. fat), 73 mg chol., 67 mg sodium, 37 g carb., 3 g dietary fiber, 25 g protein. **Daily Values:** 16 % vit. A, 15 % vit. C, 4 % calcium, 13 % iron.

CHOPS AND PINEAPPLE WITH CHILI SLAW

Start to Finish: 20 minutes | Makes: 4 servings

8 boneless top loin pork chops, about ½ inch thick (about 1½ pounds)
   Salt
1½ teaspoons chili powder
½ of a fresh pineapple, peeled, cored, and sliced
3 tablespoons cider vinegar
2 tablespoons orange juice
2 tablespoons olive oil
1 tablespoon sugar
⅓ of a small head green cabbage, cored and sliced (about 5 cups)
½ of a medium red onion, thinly sliced
1 small red sweet pepper, cut into strips
   Ground black pepper

1 Sprinkle chops lightly with salt and 1 teaspoon of the chili powder. For a charcoal grill, grill chops and pineapple slices on the rack of an uncovered grill directly over medium coals for 6 to 8 minutes or until chops are done (160°F), turning once halfway through grilling. (For a gas grill, preheat grill. Reduce heat to medium. Place chops and pineapple on grill rack over heat. Cover; grill as above.)

2 Meanwhile, for chili slaw, in a large bowl whisk together vinegar, orange juice, olive oil, sugar, and the remaining ½ teaspoon chili powder. Add cabbage, onion, and sweet pepper; toss to mix. Season with additional salt and pepper. Serve chops with pineapple slices and chili slaw.

Nutrition Facts per serving: 357 cal., 12 g total fat (3 g sat. fat), 112 mg chol., 392 mg sodium, 20 g carb., 4 g dietary fiber, 40 g protein. **Daily Values:** 27 % vit. A, 165 % vit. C, 5 % calcium, 9 % iron.

GRILLED PORK AND PINEAPPLE

Start to Finish: 18 minutes | Makes: 4 servings

- 4 **boneless top loin pork chops, ¾ inch thick (about 1¼ pounds)**
  Salt and ground black pepper
- 1 **fresh pineapple, peeled and cored**
- 3 **tablespoons orange marmalade**
- ½ **cup plain yogurt**
- ¼ **cup roasted, lightly salted cashew halves and/or pieces or toasted pecans, coarsely chopped**
  Fresh thyme (optional)

1 Sprinkle both sides of chops lightly with salt and pepper. Cut pineapple crosswise into ½-inch slices; set aside.

2 For a charcoal grill, grill chops on the rack of an uncovered grill directly over medium coals for 4 minutes. Turn; add pineapple to grill. Brush chops and pineapple with 2 tablespoons of the marmalade. Grill for 3 to 5 minutes more or until chops are done (160°F), turning pineapple once halfway through grilling. (For a gas grill, preheat grill. Reduce heat to medium. Place chops on grill rack over heat. Cover; grill as above adding pineapple as directed).

3 Meanwhile, combine yogurt and the remaining 1 tablespoon marmalade; season to taste with additional pepper.

4 Arrange chops and pineapple on 4 serving plates. Spoon yogurt mixture over chops and pineapple. Sprinkle with nuts and, if desired, garnish with thyme.

Nutrition Facts per serving: 317 cal., 7 g total fat (2 g sat. fat), 80 mg chol., 313 mg sodium, 29 g carb., 2 g dietary fiber, 35 g protein. **Daily Values:** 2 % vit. A, 72 % vit. C, 10 % calcium, 7 % iron.

MAPLE PORK AND APPLES

Start to Finish: 20 minutes | Makes: 4 servings

- 4 **bone-in pork loin chops, ½ inch thick (about 1¾ pounds)**
  Salt and ground black pepper
- 2 **tablespoons butter or margarine**
- 12 **baby carrots with tops, halved lengthwise**
- 1 **medium apple, sliced crosswise and seeds removed**
- ⅓ **cup pure maple syrup**
  Chopped pecans, toasted (optional)

1 Sprinkle chops lightly with salt and pepper. In a very large skillet melt butter over medium heat. Add chops; brown for 2 minutes, turning once. Reduce heat to medium-low. Add carrots, apple slices, and maple syrup; simmer, covered, about 8 minutes or until pork is no longer pink.

2 Using a slotted spoon, transfer chops, carrots, and apple slices to a serving platter. Bring syrup mixture in skillet to boiling. Boil gently, uncovered, for 1 to 2 minutes or until thickened. Pour over chops. If desired, sprinkle with pecans.

Nutrition Facts per serving: 451 cal., 19 g total fat (8 g sat. fat), 124 mg chol., 447 mg sodium, 25 g carb., 1 g dietary fiber, 44 g protein. **Daily Values:** 87 % vit. A, 8 % vit. C, 4 % calcium, 12 % iron.

HAM WITH CRANBERRIES AND CURRIED PEARS

Start to Finish: 18 minutes | Makes: 4 servings

3 tablespoons butter or margarine

1½ teaspoons curry powder

1 1¼-pound center-cut ham slice

1 medium sweet onion, cut into thin wedges

2 medium pears, cut into thin wedges

⅓ cup dried cranberries

1 Preheat broiler. In a large skillet melt butter over medium heat. Stir in curry powder and cook for 1 minute. Remove skillet from heat. Brush about 1 tablespoon of the curry mixture over the ham.

2 Place ham on the unheated rack of a broiler pan. Broil 4 inches from heat for 10 to 12 minutes or until heated through, turning once.

3 Meanwhile, return skillet to heat. Add onion; cook and stir for 4 minutes. Add pears and cranberries; cook for 4 to 6 minutes or just until pears are tender, stirring occasionally.

4 Divide ham into 4 portions; place on a serving platter. Spoon pear mixture on top of ham.

Nutrition Facts per serving: 307 cal., 14 g total fat (7 g sat. fat), 86 mg chol., 2395 mg sodium, 23 g carb., 4 g dietary fiber, 29 g protein. **Daily Values:** 6 % vit. A, 8 % vit. C, 2 % calcium, 3 % iron.

HAM, BRIE, AND TOMATO FRITTATA

Start to Finish: 20 minutes | Makes: 4 servings

2 tablespoons butter or margarine

8 ounces cubed cooked ham

1 small yellow summer squash, chopped

6 eggs, lightly beaten

¼ teaspoon salt

¼ teaspoon ground black pepper

½ of an 8-ounce round Brie cheese, chopped

1 large tomato, seeded and chopped

1 Preheat broiler. In a large broiler-proof skillet melt butter over medium heat. Add ham and squash; cook for 2 minutes.

2 In a medium bowl combine eggs, salt, and pepper. Add egg mixture to skillet; cook for 1 minute. Sprinkle with cheese and half of the tomato. As the mixture sets, run a spatula around edge of skillet, lifting egg mixture so uncooked portion flows underneath. Continue until egg mixture is almost set.

3 Broil 4 to 5 inches from heat about 1 minute or until top appears set. Sprinkle with remaining tomato. Cut into wedges.

Nutrition Facts per serving: 357 cal., 26 g total fat (13 g sat. fat), 393 mg chol., 1211 mg sodium, 5 g carb., 2 g dietary fiber, 25 g protein. **Daily Values:** 22 % vit. A, 15 % vit. C, 12 % calcium, 13 % iron.

HAM-VEGETABLE MEDLEY

Start to Finish: 20 minutes | Makes: 4 servings

2 medium sweet potatoes, peeled and cut into 1-inch cubes

12 ounces Brussels sprouts, trimmed and halved

2 tablespoons butter or margarine

1 to 1¼ pounds sliced cooked ham, about ¼ inch thick

½ cup apple butter

2 tablespoons cider vinegar
Salt and ground black pepper
Baguette slices (optional)

1 In a large saucepan cook sweet potatoes and Brussels sprouts in lightly salted boiling water for 8 to 10 minutes or just until tender; drain.

2 Meanwhile, in a very large skillet melt butter over medium-high heat. Add ham; cook for 4 to 5 minutes, turning occasionally. Arrange ham and vegetables on 4 serving plates; keep warm. Stir apple butter and vinegar into the skillet; heat through. Spoon over ham and vegetables. Season to taste with salt and pepper. If desired, serve with baguette slices.

Nutrition Facts per serving: 513 cal., 16 g total fat (7 g sat. fat), 80 mg chol., 1664 mg sodium, 71 g carb., 8 g dietary fiber, 23 g protein. **Daily Values:** 181 % vit. A, 104 % vit. C, 10 % calcium, 17 % iron.

WILTED CABBAGE AND BRATS

Start to Finish: 20 minutes | Makes: 4 servings

2 tablespoons olive oil

½ of a 2-pound head napa cabbage, cut into 4 wedges, leaving the core intact to hold wedges together

6 cooked smoked bratwurst links (14 to 16 ounces), halved diagonally

2 small apples, cored and cut into thin wedges

¼ cup water

2 tablespoons Dijon-style mustard

½ cup dairy sour cream or light dairy sour cream

1 tablespoon snipped fresh sage

Fresh sage leaves (optional)

1 In a very large skillet heat 1 tablespoon of the olive oil over medium heat. Add cabbage wedges; cook for 8 to 10 minutes or until light brown and tender, turning occasionally to brown evenly.

2 Meanwhile, in a 4- to 5-quart Dutch oven heat the remaining 1 tablespoon olive oil over medium-high heat. Add bratwurst and apple wedges; cook for 2 minutes. In a small bowl whisk together the water and mustard; add to bratwurst mixture. Bring to boiling; reduce heat. Simmer, covered, for 4 to 6 minutes or until apple is tender, stirring occasionally.

3 Transfer cabbage to a serving platter or bowl. Using a slotted spoon, transfer bratwurst and apple mixture to platter with cabbage. In a small bowl combine sour cream and snipped sage. Gradually whisk in bratwurst cooking juices until well combined. Spoon over bratwurst mixture. If desired, garnish with fresh sage leaves.

Nutrition Facts per serving: 456 cal., 38 g total fat (10 g sat. fat), 88 mg chol., 1046 mg sodium, 13 g carb., 2 g dietary fiber, 15 g protein. **Daily Values:** 12 % vit. A, 57 % vit. C, 13 % calcium, 8 % iron.

BRATS WITH MANGO RELISH

Start to Finish: 20 minutes | **Makes:** 4 sandwiches

1 large fresh mango, seeded, peeled, and halved

1 small red onion, cut into ½-inch slices

2 to 3 tablespoons vegetable oil

4 cooked smoked bratwurst (12 ounces)

4 hoagie buns, split

2 hearts of romaine lettuce, halved (optional)

½ teaspoon Jamaican jerk seasoning

Salt and ground black pepper

1 Brush mango and onion with 1 tablespoon of the oil.

2 For a charcoal grill, grill mango halves, onion, and bratwurst directly over medium coals about 8 minutes or until mango and bratwurst are brown and heated through and onion is crisp-tender, turning once halfway through grilling. (For a gas grill, preheat grill. Reduce heat to medium. Place mango halves, onion, and bratwurst on grill rack over heat. Cover; grill as above.) Set aside.

3 Lightly toast buns for 1 to 2 minutes on grill. If using romaine, lightly brush romaine with 1 tablespoon oil. Place romaine on grill rack directly over medium heat for 1 to 2 minutes or until light brown and wilted, turning once.

4 For relish, chop mango and onion. In a medium bowl combine mango, onion, the remaining 1 tablespoon oil, and the jerk seasoning. Season to taste with salt and pepper. Serve brats in buns with relish and romaine.

Nutrition Facts per sandwich: 478 cal., 31 g total fat (6 g sat. fat), 66 mg chol., 1112 mg sodium, 35 g carb., 2 g dietary fiber, 15 g protein. **Daily Values:** 8 % vit. A, 27 % vit. C, 8 % calcium, 13 % iron.

SWEET PEPPER PASTA WITH SAUSAGE

Start to Finish: 20 minutes | Makes: 4 servings

1　9-ounce package refrigerated linguine

1　tablespoon olive oil

1　pound frozen cooked Italian sausage links, thawed and diagonally cut into ½-inch slices

1　16-ounce package frozen (yellow, green, and red) peppers and onion stir-fry vegetables, thawed

1　15-ounce can extra thick and zesty tomato sauce

1　cup yellow and/or red pear-shape or cherry tomatoes, halved

　Finely shredded Parmesan cheese (optional)

1 Cook linguine according to package directions; drain.

2 Meanwhile, in a very large skillet heat olive oil over medium heat. Add sausage; cook and stir for 2 minutes. Add stir-fry vegetables and tomato sauce. Bring to boiling; reduce heat. Simmer, covered, for 5 minutes. Stir in tomatoes. Spoon sausage mixture over pasta. If desired, sprinkle with Parmesan cheese.

Nutrition Facts per serving: 676 cal., 36 g total fat (12 g sat. fat), 106 mg chol., 1976 mg sodium, 52 g carb., 5 g dietary fiber, 33 g protein. **Daily Values:** 22 % vit. A, 90 % vit. C, 4 % calcium, 26 % iron.

SAUSAGE AND ORZO

Start to Finish: 16 minutes | Makes: 4 servings

1　tablespoon vegetable oil

1　pound cooked sausage, halved lengthwise and cut into 2-inch pieces

1　cup dried orzo (rosamarina)

1　14-ounce can reduced-sodium beef broth

½　cup water

1　teaspoon dried Italian seasoning

2　medium zucchini, halved lengthwise and coarsely chopped (2½ cups)

⅓　cup 1-inch pieces green onion and/or finely chopped red sweet pepper

　Salt and ground black pepper

1 In a large skillet heat oil over medium-high heat. Cook sausage in hot oil about 2 minutes or until brown. Stir in orzo; cook and stir about 1 minute.

2 Stir in beef broth, the water, and Italian seasoning. Bring to boiling; reduce heat. Simmer, covered, about 8 minutes or until orzo is tender, adding the zucchini the last 4 minutes of cooking and stirring occasionally.

3 Uncover; stir in green onion and/or sweet pepper. Season to taste with salt and black pepper.

Nutrition Facts per serving: 467 cal., 24 g total fat (8 g sat. fat), 79 mg chol., 1630 mg sodium, 40 g carb., 3 g dietary fiber, 23 g protein. **Daily Values:** 6 % vit. A, 59 % vit. C, 4 % calcium, 19 % iron.

SAUCY SAUSAGE AND BEANS WITH RICE

Start to Finish: 20 minutes | **Makes:** 4 servings

1⅓ cups instant brown rice

1 16-ounce link cooked smoked sausage, halved lengthwise and cut into 1-inch pieces

1 15-ounce can chili beans in chili gravy, undrained

1 14.5-ounce can Mexican-style stewed tomatoes, undrained and cut up

1 large green sweet pepper, cut into 1-inch pieces
  Bottled hot pepper sauce (optional)

1 Cook instant rice according to package directions.

2 Meanwhile, in a large skillet cook sausage over medium heat until brown. Add undrained beans, undrained stewed tomatoes, and sweet pepper. Bring to boiling; reduce heat. Simmer, covered, for 5 to 7 minutes or until pepper is crisp-tender, stirring occasionally.

3 Divide rice among 4 plates; top with sausage mixture. If desired, pass bottled hot pepper sauce.

Nutrition Facts per serving: 717 cal., 34 g total fat (11 g sat. fat), 69 mg chol., 1556 mg sodium, 76 g carb., 11 g dietary fiber, 25 g protein. **Daily Values:** 16 % vit. A, 73 % vit. C, 7 % calcium, 25 % iron.

SAUSAGE-FRUIT KABOBS

Start to Finish: 20 minutes | **Makes:** 4 servings

3 tablespoons spicy brown or Dijon-style mustard

3 tablespoons honey

12 ounces cooked smoked sausage, diagonally cut into ½-inch slices

1 apple, cored and cut into ½-inch wedges

1 medium zucchini, halved and cut into ¼-inch slices

6 ounces crusty bread, cut into 1-inch pieces
  Olive oil

1 Preheat broiler. In a small bowl stir together mustard and honey.

2 On four 12-inch skewers alternately thread sausage, apple, and zucchini, leaving ¼ inch space between pieces. Brush with some of the mustard mixture. Set aside the remaining mustard mixture. Place kabobs on the unheated rack of a broiler pan. Broil 4 to 5 inches from the heat for 4 minutes.

3 Meanwhile, thread bread on four 12-inch skewers; lightly brush with olive oil. Add bread skewers to broiler; turn sausage skewers. Broil about 3 minutes more or until sausage is heated through and bread is toasted, turning bread once. Serve with reserved mustard mixture.

Nutrition Facts per serving: 527 cal., 32 g total fat (9 g sat. fat), 52 mg chol., 1138 mg sodium, 33 g carb., 3 g dietary fiber, 11 g protein. **Daily Values:** 2 % vit. A, 17 % vit. C, 5 % calcium, 11 % iron.

SAUSAGE-FRUIT KABOBS

POLENTA-SAUSAGE BOWL

Start to Finish: 20 minutes | **Makes:** 4 servings

- 1 **16-ounce tube refrigerated cooked polenta with sun-dried tomatoes, or plain**
- 2 **medium zucchini, halved lengthwise**
- 1 **tablespoon vegetable oil**
  Salt and ground black pepper
- 1 **pound bulk Italian sausage or ground beef**
- 1 **8-ounce package sliced fresh mushrooms**
- 1 **cup grape or cherry tomatoes**
- 1 **teaspoon dried Italian seasoning, crushed**
  Finely shredded Parmesan cheese (optional)

1 Preheat broiler. Lightly grease a baking sheet; set aside. Cut polenta into 12 slices. Place polenta and zucchini on baking sheet; brush with oil and sprinkle with salt and pepper. Broil 4 to 5 inches from the heat for 8 to 10 minutes or until polenta is light brown and zucchini is crisp-tender, turning once.

2 Meanwhile, in a very large skillet cook sausage over medium heat until sausage begins to brown; drain off fat. Add mushrooms, tomatoes, and Italian seasoning; cook about 5 minutes or until meat is no longer pink.

3 Divide polenta slices among 4 serving plates. Using a slotted spoon, spoon sausage mixture over polenta. Slice zucchini halves crosswise and serve with polenta. If desired, sprinkle with Parmesan cheese.

Nutrition Facts per serving: 547 cal., 40 g total fat (13 g sat. fat), 86 mg chol., 1340 mg sodium, 26 g carb., 3 g dietary fiber, 23 g protein. **Daily Values:** 18 % vit. A, 55 % vit. C, 5 % calcium, 15 % iron.

LAMB CHOPS WITH TOMATOES

Start to Finish: 20 minutes | **Makes:** 4 servings

- 8 lamb loin chops, 1 inch thick
  Salt and ground black pepper
- 1 8.8-ounce pouch cooked long grain rice
- 4 medium roma tomatoes, cut up
- 4 green onions, cut into 1-inch pieces
- 1 tablespoon snipped fresh oregano
- 1 tablespoon balsamic vinegar

1 Sprinkle chops lightly with salt and pepper. For a charcoal grill, grill chops on the rack of an uncovered grill directly over medium coals to desired doneness, turning once halfway through grilling. Allow 12 to 14 minutes for medium-rare (145°F) or 15 to 17 minutes for medium (160°F). (For a gas grill, preheat grill. Reduce heat to medium. Place chops on grill rack over heat. Cover; grill as above.)

2 Meanwhile, microwave rice according to package directions. In a food processor combine tomatoes, green onions, and oregano; process with on/off turns until coarsely chopped. Transfer tomato mixture to a medium bowl; stir in vinegar. Season to taste with salt and pepper. Serve chops on rice and top with tomato mixture.

Nutrition Facts per serving: 273 cal., 7 g total fat (2 g sat. fat), 70 mg chol., 153 mg sodium, 26 g carb., 3 g dietary fiber, 25 g protein. **Daily Values:** 22 % vit. A, 29 % vit. C, 4 % calcium, 15 % iron.

CHAPTER 3

FISH

SEARED SESAME SALMON

Start to Finish: 20 minutes | Makes: 4 servings

¼ cup seasoned fine dry breadcrumbs

2 tablespoons sesame seeds

4 4- to 5-ounce skinless salmon fillets, ¾ inch thick

1 tablespoon soy sauce
Salt and ground black pepper

2 to 3 tablespoons vegetable oil

12 ounces fresh asparagus spears, trimmed

¼ cup purchased hollandaise or tartar sauce

1 In a shallow dish combine breadcrumbs and sesame seeds; set aside.

2 Rinse fish; pat dry with paper towels. Brush both sides of fish with soy sauce. Sprinkle lightly with salt and pepper. Coat fish with crumb mixture.

3 In a very large skillet heat 2 tablespoons oil over medium heat. Add fish; cook for 4 minutes. Turn over; cook for 3 to 4 minutes more or until fish begins to flake when tested with a fork. Transfer fish to a serving platter; cover to keep warm.

4 Add remaining oil to skillet, if needed. Add asparagus; cook about 3 minutes or until crisp-tender, turning occasionally. Add asparagus to serving platter. Serve with hollandaise sauce.

Nutrition Facts per serving: 347 cal., 23 g total fat (4 g sat. fat), 70 mg chol., 615 mg sodium, 9 g carb., 2 g dietary fiber, 26 g protein. **Daily Values:** 9 % vit. A, 12 % vit. C, 9 % calcium, 14 % iron.

SALMON WITH MATZO CRUST

Start to Finish: 20 minutes | Oven: 450°F | Makes: 4 servings

1½ 6-inch squares matzo (1½ ounces), broken up

2 tablespoons snipped fresh dill or 1½ teaspoons dried dill

½ teaspoon salt

¼ teaspoon ground black pepper

3 tablespoons olive oil or vegetable oil

4 4- to 5-ounce skinless salmon fillets, 1 inch thick
Lemon wedges (optional)
Fresh dill sprigs (optional)
Steamed green beans (optional)

1 Preheat oven to 450°F. In a blender or food processor combine matzo, snipped dill, salt, and pepper; blend or process until coarse. Transfer crumb mixture to a sheet of waxed paper or a shallow container.

2 Brush a shallow baking pan with a little of the oil. Brush fish with some oil. Roll fish in crumb mixture to coat; place in prepared pan. Drizzle fish with remaining oil.

3 Bake, uncovered, for 10 to 12 minutes or until fish begins to flake when tested with a fork. If desired, serve with lemon wedges, fresh dill sprigs, and steamed green beans.

Nutrition Facts per serving: 340 cal., 23 g total fat (4 g sat. fat), 67 mg chol., 358 mg sodium, 9 g carb., 0 g dietary fiber, 24 g protein. **Daily Values:** 1 % vit. A, 7 % vit. C, 2 % calcium, 5 % iron.

SPICE-RUBBED SALMON

Start to Finish: 20 minutes | **Makes:** 4 servings

2 teaspoons chili powder
1 teaspoon ground cumin
1 teaspoon packed brown sugar
¼ teaspoon salt
⅛ teaspoon ground black pepper
4 5-ounce skinless salmon fillets
1 small head cabbage, cut into 6 wedges
2 to 3 tablespoons vegetable oil
1 large carrot
Salt and ground black pepper
Orange wedges

1 In a small bowl combine chili powder, cumin, brown sugar, the ¼ teaspoon salt, and the ⅛ teaspoon pepper. Measure thickness of fish. Rub fish with spice mixture. Brush cabbage wedges with 1 tablespoon of the oil.

2 For a charcoal grill, grill fish and cabbage on the greased rack of an uncovered grill directly over medium coals until fish begins to flake when tested with a fork, turning once halfway through grilling. Allow 4 to 6 minutes for each ½-inch thickness of fish. Grill cabbage for 6 to 8 minutes or until slightly charred, turning once. (For a gas grill, preheat grill. Reduce heat to medium. Place fish and cabbage on greased grill rack over heat. Cover; grill as above.)

3 Meanwhile, peel carrot and cut into wide strips. Remove fish and cabbage from grill. Coarsely chop cabbage. In a medium bowl combine cabbage, carrot, and 1 to 2 tablespoons oil. Season to taste with additional salt and pepper. Serve fish with cabbage mixture and orange wedges.

Nutrition Facts per serving: 380 cal., 23 g total fat (4 g sat. fat), 84 mg chol., 284 mg sodium, 14 g carb., 5 g dietary fiber, 31 g protein. **Daily Values:** 64 % vit. A, 122 % vit. C, 10 % calcium, 9 % iron.

SALMON WITH PEPPER RELISH

Start to Finish: 20 minutes | **Makes:** 4 servings

4 4- to 5-ounce skinless salmon fillets
Salt and ground black pepper
½ cup mango chutney (snip any large pieces)
¾ cup chopped yellow sweet pepper
½ cup chopped red onion
½ cup shredded carrot
2 tablespoons cider vinegar

1 Preheat broiler. Rinse fish; pat dry with paper towels. Measure thickness of fish. Sprinkle fish lightly with salt and pepper. Place fish on the lightly greased rack of broiler pan. Broil 4 inches from heat until fish begins to flake when tested with a fork, turning once halfway through broiling. Allow 4 to 6 minutes per ½-inch thickness of fish. Brush with ¼ cup of the chutney during the last 2 minutes of broiling time.

2 Meanwhile, for pepper relish, in a medium bowl combine the remaining ¼ cup of the chutney, the sweet pepper, red onion, carrot, and vinegar. Season to taste with salt and pepper. Serve pepper relish with fish.

Nutrition Facts per serving: 314 cal., 12 g total fat (3 g sat. fat), 67 mg chol., 484 mg sodium, 24 g carb., 1 g dietary fiber, 23 g protein. **Daily Values:** 53 % vit. A, 161 % vit. C, 3 % calcium, 4 % iron.

SALMON-POTATO CAKES

Start to Finish: 20 minutes | **Makes:** 4 servings

- **14 ounces skinless salmon fillets or one 14.75-ounce can salmon, skin and bones removed**
- **2 cups refrigerated sour cream and chive mashed potatoes**
- **½ cup seasoned fine dry breadcrumbs**
- **3 tablespoons snipped fresh dill**
- **Nonstick cooking spray**
- **1 5-ounce package mixed salad greens**
- **½ cup bottled honey Dijon salad dressing**

1 If using fresh salmon, rinse and pat dry with paper towels. Place fish in a 2-quart square baking dish. Cover with vented plastic wrap. Microwave on 100% power (high) for 2½ to 3½ minutes or until fish begins to flake when tested with a fork. Break fish into pieces with fork.

2 In a large bowl combine fish, mashed potatoes, breadcrumbs, and dill. Shape fish mixture into eight 3½-inch cakes.

3 Lightly coat a very large nonstick skillet with cooking spray. Cook cakes over medium-high heat for 3 to 4 minutes on each side or until heated through and brown. If necessary, reshape cakes with a spatula after turning.

4 Meanwhile, divide salad greens among 4 plates. Top greens with fish cakes. Serve with salad dressing.

Nutrition Facts per serving: 503 cal., 31 g total fat (7 g sat. fat), 74 mg chol., 851 mg sodium, 31 g carb., 2 g dietary fiber, 25 g protein. **Daily Values:** 17 % vit. A, 14 % vit. C, 9 % calcium, 9 % iron.

ANCHO GRILLED SALMON

Start to Finish: 20 minutes | **Makes:** 4 servings

- 2 **medium sweet potatoes**
- 1 **tablespoon sugar**
- 1 **teaspoon salt**
- 1 **teaspoon ground cumin**
- 1 **teaspoon ground ancho chile pepper or chili powder**
  Olive oil nonstick cooking spray
- 4 **5- to 6-ounce skinless salmon fillets**
- 1 **tablespoon olive oil**
- 2 **tablespoons fresh cilantro sprigs**

1 Preheat broiler. Scrub sweet potatoes. Halve potatoes lengthwise; cut into ¼-inch slices. Place sweet potato slices on the greased rack of an unheated broiler pan. In a small bowl combine sugar, salt, cumin, and ancho chile pepper. Coat both sides of potato slices with cooking spray; sprinkle both sides with half of the spice mixture. Broil 4 inches from the heat about 10 minutes or until tender, turning once halfway through cooking.

2 Meanwhile, rinse fish; pat dry with paper towels. Sprinkle fish with the remaining spice mixture. In a large skillet heat olive oil over medium heat. Cook fish in the hot oil for 8 to 12 minutes or until fish begins to flake when tested with a fork, turning once halfway through cooking.

3 Serve fish with sweet potato slices. Sprinkle with cilantro before serving.

Nutrition Facts per serving: 363 cal., 19 g total fat (4 g sat. fat), 84 mg chol., 710 mg sodium, 17 g carb., 2 g dietary fiber, 29 g protein. **Daily Values:** 193 % vit. A, 17 % vit. C, 5 % calcium, 6 % iron.

SALMON WITH FRESH CITRUS SALSA

Start to Finish: 20 minutes | **Makes:** 4 servings

4 4- to 5-ounce skinless salmon fillets, ¾ to 1 inch thick
  Salt and ground black pepper
⅓ cup red jalapeño jelly
3 medium oranges, peeled, seeded, and coarsely chopped
1 medium grapefruit, peeled and sectioned
1 cup grape or cherry tomatoes, halved

1 Preheat broiler. Sprinkle fish lightly with salt and pepper. Melt jelly in a small saucepan. Brush 2 tablespoons of the melted jelly over fish. Place fish on the unheated rack of a broiler pan. Broil 4 inches from heat for 8 to 10 minutes or until fish begins to flake when tested with a fork.

2 Meanwhile, for fresh citrus salsa, in a medium bowl combine oranges, grapefruit, tomatoes, and the remaining jelly. Season to taste with salt and pepper. Serve fish with citrus salsa.

Nutrition Facts per serving: 362 cal., 13 g total fat (3 g sat. fat), 67 mg chol., 223 mg sodium, 40 g carb., 4 g dietary fiber, 24 g protein. **Daily Values:** 27 % vit. A, 136 % vit. C, 7 % calcium, 4 % iron.

BARBECUE SALMON WITH FRESH NECTARINE SALSA

Start to Finish: 17 minutes | **Makes:** 4 servings

4 4- to 5-ounce skinless salmon fillets, about 1 inch thick
  Salt and ground black pepper
3 tablespoons bottled barbecue sauce
2 nectarines, pitted and chopped
¾ cup fresh blueberries
¼ cup coarsely chopped pecans, toasted
  Lemon wedges

1 Rinse fish; pat dry with paper towels. Sprinkle fish lightly with salt and pepper. Place 2 tablespoons of the barbecue sauce in a small bowl; brush both sides of fish with sauce.

2 For a charcoal grill, grill fish on the greased grill rack of an uncovered grill directly over medium coals for 8 to 12 minutes or until fish begins to flake when tested with a fork, turning once halfway through grilling. (For gas grill, preheat grill. Reduce heat to medium. Place fish on greased grill rack over medium heat. Cover and grill as above.)

3 For nectarine salsa, in a medium bowl combine nectarines, blueberries, pecans, and the remaining 1 tablespoon barbecue sauce. Season to taste with salt. Serve salmon with nectarine salsa and lemon wedges.

Nutrition Facts per serving: 318 cal., 17 g total fat (3 g sat. fat), 66 mg chol., 344 mg sodium, 17 g carb., 3 g dietary fiber, 24 g protein. **Daily Values:** 6 % vit. A, 20 % vit. C, 3 % calcium, 5 % iron.

BARBECUE SALMON WITH FRESH NECTARINE SALSA

SALMON AND NOODLE BOWL

Start to Finish: 20 minutes | **Makes:** 4 servings

1 **9-ounce package refrigerated fettuccine**
1 **pound skinless, boneless 1-inch thick salmon fillet, cut into 8 pieces**
2 **tablespoons olive oil**
  Salt and ground black pepper
6 **cups packaged fresh baby spinach**
½ **cup bottled roasted red or yellow sweet peppers**
½ **cup garlic-stuffed green olives, coarsely chopped (optional)**
½ **cup reduced-calorie balsamic vinaigrette salad dressing**

1 Cook pasta according to package directions.

2 Meanwhile, brush fish with 1 tablespoon of the olive oil. Sprinkle fish lightly with salt and black pepper. Heat a very large skillet over medium heat. Add fish to hot skillet; cook for 8 to 12 minutes or until fish begins to flake when tested with a fork, turning once halfway through cooking. Remove fish from skillet; cover and keep warm.

3 Add spinach, roasted peppers, olives (if desired), and the remaining 1 tablespoon olive oil to skillet; cook and stir for 1 for 2 minutes or just until spinach is wilted. Drain pasta; add to skillet. Add dressing; toss to coat. Season to taste with salt and black pepper.

4 Divide pasta mixture among 4 shallow bowls; top with fish.

Nutrition Facts per serving: 508 cal., 25 g total fat (5 g sat. fat), 108 mg chol., 733 mg sodium, 39 g carb., 3 g dietary fiber, 31 g protein. **Daily Values:** 86 % vit. A, 113 % vit. C, 7 % calcium, 18 % iron.

SALMON WITH WILTED SPINACH

Start to Finish: 20 minutes | **Makes:** 4 servings

1 **1-pound salmon fillet**
1 **tablespoon bottled Asian salad dressing, such as sesame ginger**
6 **cups baby spinach leaves**
1 **medium orange, peeled and sectioned**
½ **cup bottled Asian salad dressing, such as sesame ginger**

1 Preheat broiler. Rinse fish; pat dry with paper towels. Measure thickness of fish. Cut fish into 4 pieces. Place fish on the lightly greased rack of a broiler pan. Broil 4 inches from the heat until fish begins to flake when tested with a fork, turning once and brushing with the 1 tablespoon salad dressing halfway through broiling. Allow 4 to 6 minutes per ½-inch thickness of fish. Cover; keep warm.

2 In a salad bowl combine spinach and orange sections. In a large skillet bring the ½ cup salad dressing to boiling. Boil gently, uncovered, for 1 minute. Pour hot dressing over greens; toss to coat.

3 Divide greens among 4 plates. Top with fish; serve immediately.

Nutrition Facts per serving: 397 cal., 25 g total fat (5 g sat. fat), 67 mg chol., 623 mg sodium, 20 g carb., 3 g dietary fiber, 24 g protein. **Daily Values:** 12 % vit. A, 69 % vit. C, 6 % calcium, 5 % iron.

SALMON AND NOODLE BOWL

PEPPERED SALMON WITH QUICK RATATOUILLE

Start to Finish: 20 minutes | **Oven:** 450°F | **Makes:** 4 servings

4 6-ounce skinless salmon fillets

Salt and freshly ground black pepper

2 tablespoons vegetable oil

1 large red sweet onion, cut into thin wedges

2 medium zucchini, halved lengthwise and cut into 1-inch pieces

1 small eggplant, peeled and cubed

1 14.5-ounce can Italian-style stewed tomatoes, undrained

1 Preheat oven to 450°F. Measure thickness of fish. Sprinkle fish lightly with salt; sprinkle generously with pepper. Place fish on a baking sheet. Bake until fish begins to flake when tested with a fork. Allow 4 to 6 minutes per ½-inch thickness of fish.

2 Meanwhile, in a very large skillet heat oil over medium-high heat. Add onion to skillet; cook for 2 minutes. Add zucchini, eggplant, and undrained tomatoes. Bring to boiling; reduce heat. Simmer, covered, for 5 minutes. Serve vegetable mixture with fish.

Nutrition Facts per serving: 450 cal., 26 g total fat (5 g sat. fat), 100 mg chol., 601 mg sodium, 19 g carb., 7 g dietary fiber, 37 g protein. **Daily Values:** 14 % vit. A, 58 % vit. C, 7 % calcium, 9 % iron.

TUNA-POTATO CAKES

Start to Finish: 18 minutes | Makes: 4 servings

- 1 cup packaged refrigerated mashed potatoes with garlic*
- 1 12-ounce can tuna (water pack), drained and broken into chunks
- 1/3 cup seasoned fine dry breadcrumbs
- 1/2 cup finely chopped celery (1 stalk)
- 1/4 teaspoon ground black pepper
- 2 tablespoons vegetable oil
- 1/4 cup purchased tartar sauce

1 In a medium bowl combine mashed potatoes, tuna, breadcrumbs, celery, and pepper.

2 In a large skillet heat oil over medium heat. Drop about 1/3 cup tuna mixture into hot oil flattening to 1/2-inch patty; cook about 4 minutes or until brown. Carefully turn; cook about 4 minutes more. Repeat with remaining mixture. Serve with tartar sauce.

Nutrition Facts per serving: 267 cal., 14 g total fat (2 g sat. fat), 22 mg chol., 621 mg sodium, 16 g carb., 1 g dietary fiber, 19 g protein. **Daily Values:** 2 % vit. A, 16 % vit. C, 3 % calcium, 8 % iron.

*TIP: Instead of packaged refrigerated mashed potatoes, use leftover mashed potatoes plus 1/4 teaspoon garlic powder.

SPICY CATFISH WITH QUICK CUCUMBER SALSA

Start to Finish: 20 minutes | Makes: 4 servings

- 4 4- to 5-ounce catfish fillets
- 2 teaspoons Szechuan-style pepper blend
- 1/2 teaspoon salt
- 1 large cucumber, seeded and chopped
- 3/4 cup chopped green sweet pepper
- 1 1/2 cups cherry tomatoes, quartered

1 Preheat broiler. Rinse fish; pat dry with paper towels. Measure thickness of fish. Combine pepper blend and salt in a small bowl. Sprinkle fish with half of the seasoning mixture. Place fish on the unheated rack of a broiler pan.

2 Broil fish 4 inches from heat until fish begins to flake when tested with a fork. Allow 4 to 6 minutes per 1/2-inch thickness of fish.

3 Meanwhile, for cucumber salsa, in a medium bowl combine cucumber, sweet pepper, tomatoes, and the remaining seasoning mixture.

4 Serve fish with cucumber salsa.

Nutrition Facts per serving: 189 cal., 9 g total fat (2 g sat. fat), 53 mg chol., 358 mg sodium, 8 g carb., 2 g dietary fiber, 19 g protein. **Daily Values:** 17 % vit. A, 60 % vit. C, 4 % calcium, 8 % iron.

CATFISH WITH SUMMER SUCCOTASH

Start to Finish: 20 minutes | Makes: 4 servings

2 cups frozen lima beans
4 4- to 6-ounce catfish fillets, about ½ inch thick
Olive oil
Garlic salt
Ground black pepper
1 cup purchased corn relish
1 cup fresh baby spinach

1 Cook lima beans according to package directions. Drain in a colander; rinse under cold water to cool quickly.

2 Meanwhile, rinse fish; pat dry with paper towels. Brush fish with olive oil. Sprinkle with garlic salt and pepper. Place fish in a well-greased grill basket. For a charcoal grill, place grill basket on the grill rack of an uncovered grill directly over medium coals. Grill for 6 to 9 minutes or until fish begins to flake when tested with a fork, turning basket once halfway through grilling. (For a gas grill, preheat grill. Reduce heat to medium. Place grill basket on grill rack directly over heat; cover and grill as above.)

3 Place fish on serving platter. For succotash, in a large bowl toss together cooked lima beans, corn relish, and spinach. Serve succotash with fish.

Nutrition Facts per serving: 372 cal., 12 g total fat (3 g sat. fat), 53 mg chol., 509 mg sodium, 41 g carb., 5 g dietary fiber, 24 g protein. **Daily Values:** 18 % vit. A, 16 % vit. C, 5 % calcium, 15 % iron.

TILAPIA WITH GRAPE CHUTNEY

Start to Finish: 20 minutes | Makes: 4 servings

4 4-ounce skinless tilapia or sole fillets
Salt and ground black pepper
2 tablespoons vegetable oil
1 cup seedless green grapes
½ cup tropical blend mixed dried fruit bits
⅓ cup sliced green onion
⅓ cup apricot spreadable fruit
Cooked brown rice (optional)

1 Rinse fish; pat dry with paper towels. Sprinkle fish lightly with salt and pepper.

2 In a very large skillet heat oil over medium-high heat. Add fish; cook for 3 to 4 minutes or until fish begins to flake when tested with a fork, turning once halfway through cooking.

3 Meanwhile, cut grapes into halves.

4 Transfer fish to platter; keep warm. For grape chutney, add grapes, fruit bits, green onion, and spreadable fruit to skillet; cook and stir for 2 minutes. Season to taste with salt and pepper. Serve chutney over fish. If desired, serve with hot cooked brown rice.

Nutrition Facts per serving: 305 cal., 9 g total fat (1 g sat. fat), 57 mg chol., 208 mg sodium, 37 g carb., 2 g dietary fiber, 24 g protein. **Daily Values:** 10 % vit. A, 10 % vit. C, 3 % calcium, 8 % iron.

CATFISH WITH SUMMER SUCCOTASH

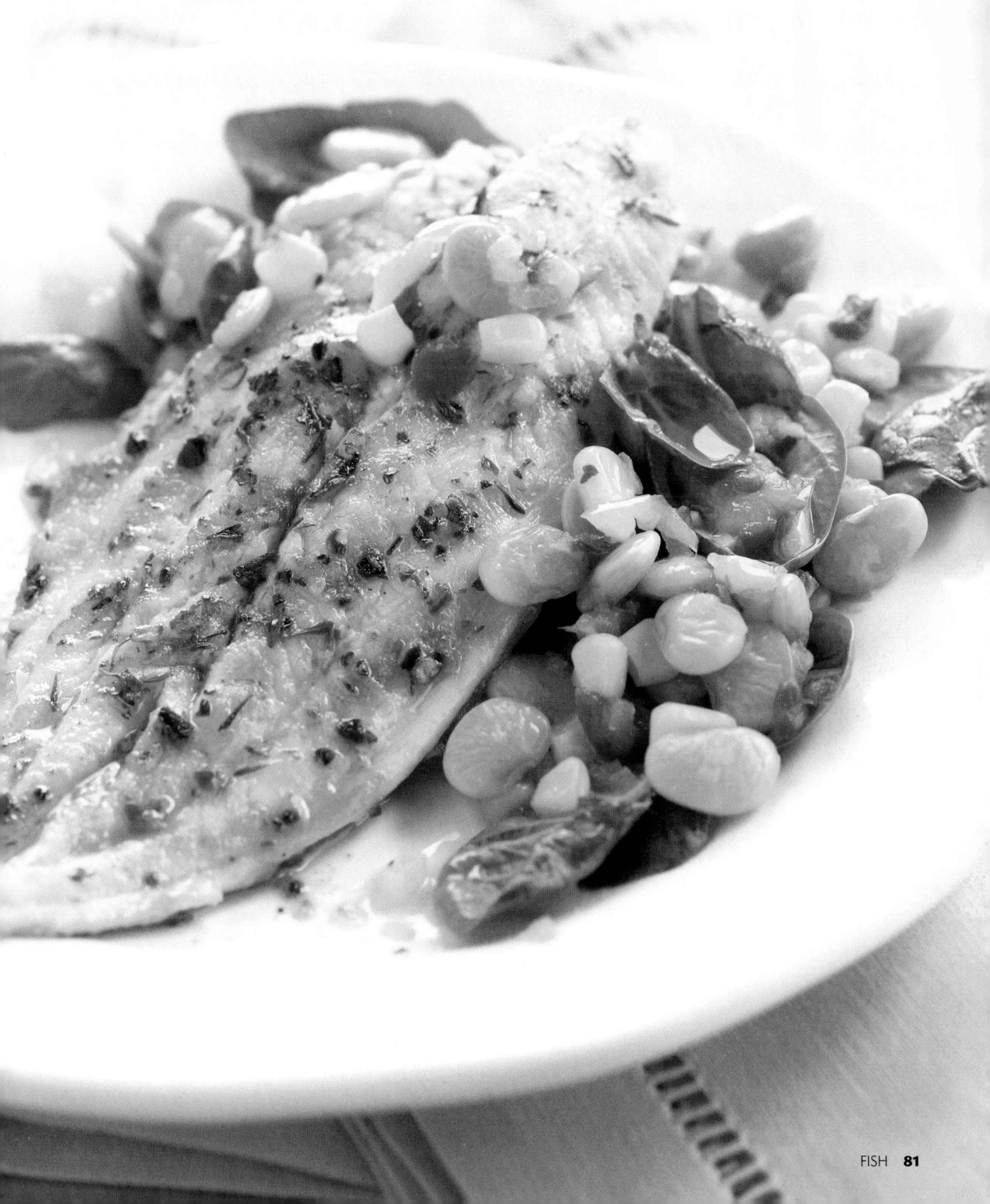

GINGER TILAPIA

Start to Finish: 20 minutes | Makes: 4 servings

½ cup cider vinegar
¼ cup packed brown sugar
2 teaspoons grated fresh ginger
½ teaspoon salt
2 medium cucumbers, sliced (about 3½ cups)
2 tablespoons coarsely chopped fresh mint
4 4-ounce tilapia fillets, ½ to ¾ inch thick
   Nonstick cooking spray
1 6-ounce container plain yogurt
1 teaspoon packed brown sugar
   Lemon peel strips (optional)
   Cracked black pepper (optional)
   Lemon wedges (optional)

1 Preheat broiler. In a medium bowl stir together vinegar, the ¼ cup brown sugar, the ginger, and salt until sugar dissolves. Remove ¼ cup of the mixture. Add cucumber and 1 tablespoon of the mint to the remaining mixture; toss to coat and set aside.

2 Rinse fish; pat dry with paper towels. Lightly coat the rack of an unheated broiler pan with cooking spray; place fish on broiler pan. Brush the ¼ cup vinegar mixture over the fish. Broil 4 inches from the heat for 4 to 6 minutes or until fish begins to flake when tested with a fork.

3 Meanwhile, in another small bowl combine yogurt, the remaining 1 tablespoon mint, and the 1 teaspoon brown sugar.

4 Using a slotted spoon, divide cucumber slices among 4 plates. Top with fish and yogurt mixture. If desired, top with lemon peel strips and cracked pepper and serve with lemon wedges.

Nutrition Facts per serving: 210 cal., 3 g total fat (1 g sat. fat), 59 mg chol., 388 mg sodium, 23 g carb., 0 g dietary fiber, 26 g protein. **Daily Values:** 2 % vit. A, 8 % vit. C, 12 % calcium, 10 % iron.

TILAPIA ON MELON

Start to Finish: 20 minutes | Makes: 4 servings

- 1 pound tilapia fillets
- 1 tablespoon olive oil
- 1½ teaspoons lemon-pepper seasoning
- ½ of a small cantaloupe
- 1 medium cucumber, thinly sliced
- ⅓ cup plain low-fat yogurt
- 1 tablespoon honey

1 Preheat broiler. Rinse fish; pat dry with paper towels. Cut fish into 4 serving-size pieces, if needed. Measure thickness of fish. Brush fish with olive oil; sprinkle with ¾ teaspoon lemon-pepper seasoning. Place fish on the rack of an unheated broiler pan.

2 Broil fish 3 to 4 inches from heat until fish begins to flake when tested with a fork. Allow 4 to 6 minutes per ½-inch thickness of fish.

3 Meanwhile, peel and seed cantaloupe; cut into thin slices. Arrange cantaloupe and cucumber on a large serving platter. Top with fish. For sauce, in a small bowl combine yogurt, honey, and the remaining ¾ teaspoon lemon-pepper seasoning. Serve sauce over fish and melon mixture.

Nutrition Facts per serving: 204 cal., 6 g total fat (2 g sat. fat), 58 mg chol., 493 mg sodium, 14 g carb., 1 g dietary fiber, 25 g protein. **Daily Values:** 48 % vit. A, 46 % vit. C, 7 % calcium, 6 % iron.

POACHED COD IN ORANGE SAUCE

Start to Finish: 20 minutes | Makes: 4 servings

- ¼ cup sliced almonds
- 1 cup orange juice
- 4 4- to 5-ounce cod fillets, about ¾ inch thick
  Salt and ground black pepper
- 12 ounces fresh asparagus spears, trimmed
- 1 medium pear, peeled, cored, and cut into wedges
- 1½ cups water
- ¼ teaspoon salt
- 1 cup quick-cooking couscous
- 1½ teaspoon cornstarch

1 Heat a very large skillet over medium heat. Add almonds; cook and stir for 2 to 3 minutes or until lightly toasted. Remove almonds from skillet; set aside.

2 Reserve 2 tablespoons of the orange juice. Add remaining orange juice to the skillet; bring to boiling. Rinse fish; pat dry with paper towels and sprinkle lightly with salt and pepper. Add fish, asparagus, and pear to skillet. Return to boiling; reduce heat. Simmer, covered, for 6 to 8 minutes or until fish begins to flake when tested with a fork.

3 Meanwhile, in a medium saucepan bring the water and the ¼ teaspoon salt to boiling. Remove saucepan from heat; add couscous. Cover and let stand for 5 minutes. Spoon couscous onto a serving platter. Using a slotted spoon, transfer fish, asparagus, and pear to platter. Keep warm.

4 For orange sauce, strain orange juice mixture and return to skillet. In a small bowl combine the reserved 2 tablespoons orange juice and the cornstarch; stir into mixture in skillet. Cook and stir until thickened and bubbly; cook and stir for 2 minutes more. Spoon sauce over fish and vegetables.

Nutrition Facts per serving: 539 cal., 4 g total fat (1 g sat. fat), 49 mg chol., 363 mg sodium, 89 g carb., 8 g dietary fiber, 35 g protein. **Daily Values:** 12 % vit. A, 62 % vit. C, 8 % calcium, 17 % iron.

SESAME-CRUSTED COD

Start to Finish: 20 minutes | Makes: 4 servings

1 pound cod fillets, ¾ inch thick
  Salt and ground black pepper
2 tablespoons sesame seeds
3 tablespoons butter or margarine, melted
1 12-ounce package trimmed fresh tender young green beans
1 medium orange, halved and sliced
3 cloves garlic, thinly sliced

1 Preheat broiler. Rinse fish; pat dry with paper towels. Cut fish into 4 serving-size pieces, if needed. Place fish on the unheated rack of a broiler pan. Sprinkle fish lightly with salt and pepper. Stir sesame seeds into the melted butter. Reserve 1 tablespoon of the butter mixture. Brush fish with half of the remaining butter mixture.

2 Broil fish 5 to 6 inches from heat for 4 minutes; turn fish. Brush with the remaining half of the butter mixture. Broil for 5 to 6 minutes more or until fish begins to flake when tested with a fork.

3 Meanwhile, in a very large skillet heat the reserved 1 tablespoon butter mixture over medium-high heat. Add green beans and orange slices; cover and cook for 2 minutes. Uncover; add garlic; cook, uncovered, for 5 to 6 minutes more or until beans are crisp-tender, stirring frequently. Serve bean mixture with fish.

Nutrition Facts per serving: 241 cal., 12 g total fat (6 g sat. fat), 72 mg chol., 274 mg sodium, 12 g carb., 4 g dietary fiber, 23 g protein. **Daily Values:** 19 % vit. A, 55 % vit. C, 11 % calcium, 12 % iron.

ITALIAN FISH FILLETS

Start to Finish: 20 minutes | Makes: 4 servings

1 pound cod fillets
  Salt and ground black pepper
2 tablespoons vegetable oil
1 14.5-ounce can Italian-style stewed tomatoes, undrained
2 medium zucchini, halved lengthwise and sliced
1 9-ounce package frozen artichoke hearts
1 14.8-ounce pouch cooked long grain white rice

1 Rinse fish; pat dry with paper towels. Sprinkle fish lightly with salt and pepper. In a very large skillet heat oil over medium-high heat. Add fish; cook for 2 minutes per side. Add undrained tomatoes, zucchini, and artichokes. Bring to boiling; reduce heat. Simmer, covered, for 6 to 8 minutes or until fish begins to flake when tested with a fork and zucchini is tender.

2 Meanwhile, prepare rice according to package directions. Serve rice with fish and vegetables.

Nutrition Facts per serving: 388 cal., 10 g total fat (1 g sat. fat), 49 mg chol., 500 mg sodium, 48 g carb., 8 g dietary fiber, 26 g protein. **Daily Values:** 16 % vit. A, 56 % vit. C, 10 % calcium, 14 % iron.

PARMESAN-CRUSTED FISH

Start to Finish: 20 minutes | **Oven:** 450°F | **Makes:** 4 servings

Nonstick cooking spray
4 skinless cod fillets
Salt and ground black pepper
1/3 cup panko (Japanese-style) breadcrumbs
1/4 cup finely shredded Parmesan cheese
1/2 cup water
1 10-ounce package julienne or shredded fresh carrot (3 cups)
1 tablespoon butter or margarine
3/4 teaspoon ground ginger
Mixed salad greens (optional)

1 Preheat oven to 450°F. Lightly coat a baking sheet with cooking spray. Rinse fish; pat dry with paper towels. Measure thickness of fish. Arrange fish on baking sheet. Sprinkle fish lightly with salt and pepper. In a small bowl combine breadcrumbs and Parmesan cheese. Sprinkle over fish.

2 Bake, uncovered, until crumbs are golden brown and fish begins to flake when tested with a fork. Allow for 4 to 6 minutes per ½-inch thickness of fish.

3 Meanwhile, in a large skillet bring the water to boiling. Add carrot; reduce heat to medium. Cook, covered, for 5 minutes. Uncover and cook about 2 minutes more or until water evaporates. Add butter and ginger; toss until butter melts and carrot is coated. Season to taste with salt and pepper. Serve fish with carrot mixture and, if desired, greens.

Nutrition Facts per serving: 233 cal., 6 g total fat (3 g sat. fat), 84 mg chol., 407 mg sodium, 11 g carb., 2 g dietary fiber, 34 g protein. **Daily Values:** 242 % vit. A, 9 % vit. C, 12 % calcium, 5 % iron.

PEANUT-SAUCED SHRIMP AND NOODLES

Start to Finish: 20 minutes | **Makes:** 4 servings

½ **of a 14-ounce package dried medium rice noodles**

4 **cups water**

1 **tablespoon vegetable oil**

12 **ounces peeled, deveined uncooked medium shrimp**

12 **ounces asparagus spears, trimmed and cut into 2-inch pieces (3 cups)**

1 **large red or yellow sweet pepper, cut in ¾-inch pieces (1 cup)**

½ **cup bottled peanut sauce**

1 Place noodles in a large bowl. Bring the water to boiling; pour boiling water over noodles in bowl. Let stand for 10 minutes.

2 Meanwhile, in a large skillet heat oil over medium-high heat. Add shrimp, asparagus, and sweet pepper; cook and stir for 3 to 5 minutes or until shrimp are opaque. Stir in peanut sauce; heat through.

3 Drain noodles. Divide noodles among 4 shallow serving bowls, using a fork to twist noodles into nest. Top with shrimp, asparagus, and sweet pepper mixture.

Nutrition Facts per serving: 396 cal., 9 g total fat (2 g sat. fat), 129 mg chol., 642 mg sodium, 55 g carb., 5 g dietary fiber, 21 g protein. **Daily Values:** 34 % vit. A, 88 % vit. C, 7 % calcium, 22 % iron.

GARLICKY PEPPERS AND SHRIMP

Start to Finish: 20 minutes | Makes: 4 servings

1 9-ounce package refrigerated spinach or plain fettuccine
4 tablespoons olive oil
3 small red, green, yellow, and/or orange sweet peppers, seeded and cut into thin strips
2 medium onions, cut into thin wedges
4 cloves garlic, thinly sliced
1 pound peeled, deveined uncooked medium shrimp
⅛ teaspoon cayenne pepper
1 cup small fresh basil leaves (optional)

1 Cook pasta according to package directions; drain and return to pan. Toss with 2 tablespoons of the olive oil; keep warm.

2 Meanwhile, in a very large skillet heat the remaining 2 tablespoons olive oil over medium-high heat. Stir in sweet peppers, onions, and garlic; stir-fry for 4 to 6 minutes or until crisp-tender. Add shrimp and cayenne pepper; cook for 2 to 3 minutes or until shrimp are opaque, stirring occasionally.

3 Serve shrimp mixture over pasta. If desired, sprinkle with basil.

Nutrition Facts per serving: 477 cal., 18 g total fat (3 g sat. fat), 229 mg chol., 256 mg sodium, 45 g carb., 4 g dietary fiber, 33 g protein. **Daily Values:** 46 % vit. A, 140 % vit. C, 13 % calcium, 29 % iron.

QUICK COCONUT SHRIMP

Start to Finish: 20 minutes | Oven: 450°F | Makes: 4 servings

Nonstick cooking spray
1 pound peeled, deveined uncooked large shrimp
Salt and ground black pepper
⅓ cup bottled sweet-and-sour sauce
1½ cups shredded coconut
2 medium yellow summer squash

1 Preheat oven to 450°F. Lightly coat a baking sheet and a 15x10x1-inch baking pan with cooking spray; set aside. Sprinkle shrimp lightly with salt and pepper. Place sweet-and-sour sauce in a medium bowl; place coconut in a small bowl. Add shrimp to bowl with sauce and stir to coat. Add shrimp, a few at a time, to dish with coconut; turn shrimp to coat. Arrange shrimp in a single layer on the prepared baking sheet.

2 Trim ends from squash; cut into ½-inch slices. Arrange squash in a single layer in the prepared pan. Sprinkle with salt and pepper; lightly coat with cooking spray.

3 Bake for 8 to 10 minutes or until shrimp are opaque and squash is tender. Serve shrimp with squash slices.

Nutrition Facts per serving: 380 cal., 17 g total fat (14 g sat. fat), 172 mg chol., 659 mg sodium, 31 g carb., 4 g dietary fiber, 27 g protein. **Daily Values:** 6 % vit. A, 12 % vit. C, 7 % calcium, 17 % iron.

SWEET-SOUR LEMON SHRIMP LO MEIN

Start to Finish: 16 minutes | Makes: 4 servings

- 2 3-ounce packages ramen noodles (any flavor)
- 1 pound peeled, deveined uncooked shrimp
- 1 tablespoon cornstarch
- 2 tablespoons vegetable oil
- 2 medium red, green, and/or yellow sweet peppers, cut into bite-size strips
- 1 cup snow pea pods, trimmed and halved crosswise
- ½ cup water
- ¼ cup frozen lemonade concentrate, thawed
- 1 tablespoon cider vinegar
- 1 tablespoon soy sauce

1 Discard seasoning packet from ramen noodles. Break up noodles slightly; cook according to package directions. Drain.

2 Meanwhile, in a large bowl toss shrimp with cornstarch. In a very large skillet heat oil over medium-high heat. Add sweet peppers; cook and stir for 2 minutes. Add shrimp and pea pods; cook and stir about 3 minutes more or until shrimp are opaque. Add the water, lemonade concentrate, vinegar, and soy sauce; bring to boiling. Stir in noodles; cook and stir for 1 minute to heat through.

Nutrition Facts per serving: 439 cal., 16 g total fat (5 g sat. fat), 172 mg chol., 500 mg sodium, 43 g carb., 3 g dietary fiber, 29 g protein. **Daily Values:** 44 % vit. A, 151 % vit. C, 7 % calcium, 26 % iron.

SAUCY SHRIMP AND VEGGIES

Start to Finish: 20 minutes | Makes: 4 servings

- 1 12-ounce package peeled fresh baby carrots
- 8 ounces broccoli, trimmed and cut up (3 cups)
- 1 tablespoon vegetable oil
- 1 pound peeled, deveined uncooked medium shrimp
- 1 cup cherry tomatoes
- ⅓ cup honey
- 2 tablespoons bottled chili-garlic sauce
- 2 tablespoons orange juice

1 In a large saucepan cook baby carrots, covered, in boiling lightly salted water for 5 minutes. Add broccoli; cook for 3 to 4 minutes more or just until vegetables are tender. Drain.

2 Meanwhile, heat oil in a large skillet over medium-high heat. Add shrimp and tomatoes; cook and stir for 3 to 4 minutes or until shrimp are opaque. Transfer shrimp mixture to a serving platter; add vegetable mixture to the platter.

3 For sauce, in the same skillet combine honey, chili sauce, and orange juice; heat through. Spoon over shrimp and vegetable mixtures.

Nutrition Facts per serving: 319 cal., 6 g total fat (1 g sat. fat), 172 mg chol., 361 mg sodium, 43 g carb., 5 g dietary fiber, 26 g protein. **Daily Values:** 254 % vit. A, 127 % vit. C, 13 % calcium, 23 % iron.

SAUCY SHRIMP AND VEGGIES

CHAPTER 4

MEATLESS MEALS

QUICK FETTUCCINE FLORENTINE

Start to Finish: 17 minutes | Makes: 4 servings

1 9-ounce package refrigerated fettuccine, cut into 4-inch lengths

1 15-ounce can cannellini (white kidney) beans, rinsed and drained

3 tablespoons olive oil

4 cups fresh baby spinach

½ cup bottled roasted red sweet peppers, chopped

1 cup finely shredded Romano cheese (4 ounces)

1 In a Dutch oven cook pasta according to package directions; drain. Return pasta to pan.

2 Stir drained beans and olive oil into pasta in pan; cook and stir until heated through. Add spinach and roasted peppers; toss over medium heat just until spinach begins to wilt. Serve immediately; sprinkle with Romano cheese.

Nutrition Facts per serving: 441 cal., 18 g total fat (6 g sat. fat), 62 mg chol., 557 mg sodium, 53 g carb., 7 g dietary fiber, 21 g protein. **Daily Values:** 58 % vit. A, 99 % vit. C, 31 % calcium, 23 % iron.

GREEK PASTA TOSS

Start to Finish: 18 minutes | Makes: 4 servings

1 9-ounce package refrigerated cheese-filled spinach tortellini

1 15-ounce can cannellini (white kidney) beans, rinsed and drained

¾ cup crumbled garlic-and-herb-flavored feta cheese (3 ounces)

2 tablespoons olive oil

1 large tomato, chopped Ground black pepper

4 cups fresh baby spinach

1 Cook pasta according to package directions; drain. Return pasta to pan.

2 Add drained beans, cheese, and olive oil to pasta in pan; cook over medium heat until beans are hot and cheese begins to melt, gently stirring occasionally. Add tomato; cook for 1 minute more. Season to taste with pepper.

3 Divide spinach among 4 plates; top with pasta mixture.

Nutrition Facts per serving: 448 cal., 18 g total fat (7 g sat. fat), 60 mg chol., 858 mg sodium, 55 g carb., 9 g dietary fiber, 24 g protein. **Daily Values:** 69 % vit. A, 21 % vit. C, 28 % calcium, 19 % iron.

GREEK PASTA TOSS

RAVIOLI WITH SPINACH PESTO

RAVIOLI WITH SPINACH PESTO

Start to Finish: 20 minutes | Makes: 4 servings

- 1 9-ounce package refrigerated four-cheese ravioli or tortellini
- 12 ounces baby pattypan squash, halved, or yellow summer squash, halved lengthwise and cut into ½-inch slices
- 3½ cups fresh baby spinach
- ½ cup torn fresh basil
- ¼ cup bottled Caesar Parmesan vinaigrette salad dressing
- 2 tablespoons water
  Shredded Parmesan cheese (optional)

1 Cook ravioli according to package directions, adding squash for the last 2 minutes of cooking; drain.

2 Meanwhile, for pesto, in a blender combine spinach, basil, salad dressing, and the water. Cover and blend until smooth, stopping to scrape down blender as needed.

3 Toss ravioli mixture with pesto. If desired, sprinkle with Parmesan cheese.

Nutrition Facts per serving: 218 cal., 6 g total fat (2 g sat. fat), 27 mg chol., 525 mg sodium, 31 g carb., 3 g dietary fiber, 11 g protein. **Daily Values:** 58 % vit. A, 38 % vit. C, 13 % calcium, 12 % iron.

RAVIOLI WITH ZUCCHINI

Start to Finish: 18 minutes | Makes: 4 servings

- 1 9-ounce package refrigerated whole wheat or plain cheese ravioli
- 2 tablespoons olive oil
- ½ cup walnuts, coarsely chopped
- 2 medium zucchini, halved lengthwise and sliced
- 6 green onions, diagonally sliced ¼ inch thick
- ⅓ cup milk
- 1 cup finely shredded Parmesan cheese (4 ounces)
- ⅛ teaspoon salt
- ⅛ teaspoon ground black pepper

1 Cook ravioli in 4 cups boiling lightly salted water for 6 to 8 minutes or until tender; drain.

2 Meanwhile, in a large skillet heat oil over medium heat. Add walnuts; cook and stir for 2 to 3 minutes or until toasted. Remove walnuts with a slotted spoon. Add zucchini and green onions; cook and stir for 2 to 3 minutes or until crisp-tender.

3 Add cooked pasta, walnuts, milk, and ¾ cup of the Parmesan cheese to skillet; cook and toss for 1 minute. Season with salt and pepper. Transfer to a serving bowl; sprinkle with the remaining ¼ cup cheese.

Nutrition Facts per serving: 466 cal., 29 g total fat (9 g sat. fat), 59 mg chol., 859 mg sodium, 33 g carb., 6 g dietary fiber, 21 g protein. **Daily Values:** 12 % vit. A, 35 % vit. C, 41 % calcium, 14 % iron.

PASTA WITH SPINACH AND EDAMAME

Start to Finish: 20 minutes | Makes: 4 servings

1 9-ounce package refrigerated fettuccine

2 cups frozen sweet soybeans (edamame)

½ cup walnuts, broken

⅔ cup bottled Italian salad dressing with cheese

¼ teaspoon ground black pepper

4 cups fresh baby spinach
Finely shredded Parmesan cheese (optional)

1 In a Dutch oven cook pasta and soybeans according to pasta package directions; drain. Return pasta and soybeans to pan.

2 Meanwhile, in a medium skillet toast walnuts over medium heat for 3 to 4 minutes. Remove from heat; set aside.

3 Stir salad dressing and pepper into hot pasta mixture in pan. Add spinach and nuts; cook and toss over medium heat for 1 minute more. If desired, sprinkle with Parmesan cheese.

Nutrition Facts per serving: 498 cal., 28 g total fat (4 g sat. fat), 48 mg chol., 526 mg sodium, 47 g carb., 7 g dietary fiber, 20 g protein. Daily Values: 56 % vit. A, 22 % vit. C, 11 % calcium, 24 % iron.

TORTELLINI STIR-FRY

Start to Finish: 20 minutes | Makes: 4 servings

1 9-ounce package refrigerated cheese-filled tortellini

1 tablespoon vegetable oil

1 16-ounce package fresh cut or frozen stir-fry vegetables (such as broccoli, pea pods, carrots, and celery)

¾ cup peanut stir-fry sauce

¼ cup dry-roasted cashews, chopped

1 Cook tortellini according to package directions; drain.

2 In wok or large skillet heat oil over medium-high heat. Add stir-fry vegetables; cook and stir for 3 to 5 minutes (7 to 8 minutes for frozen vegetables) or until crisp-tender. Add tortellini and stir-fry sauce; toss gently to coat. Heat through. Sprinkle with cashews; serve immediately.

Nutrition Facts per serving: 400 cal., 16 g total fat (3 g sat. fat), 30 mg chol., 1256 mg sodium, 48 g carb., 4 g dietary fiber, 18 g protein. Daily Values: 30 % vit. A, 42 % vit. C, 13 % calcium, 14 % iron.

TIP: Vary this recipe every time by choosing a different vegetable blend and different sauce.

TORTELLINI STIR-FRY

SWEET POTATO AND BLACK BEAN COUSCOUS

Start to Finish: 20 minutes | **Makes:** 4 servings

1 medium sweet potato, peeled and cubed (about 8 ounces)
1 medium green sweet pepper, cut into bite-size strips
2 cups water
1 16-ounce jar pineapple salsa
1 15- to 16-ounce can black beans, rinsed and drained
1 cup quick-cooking couscous

1 In a medium saucepan combine sweet potato, sweet pepper, and ½ cup of the water. Heat to boiling; reduce heat. Simmer, covered, for 8 to 10 minutes or until sweet potato is tender. Add pineapple salsa and drained beans; heat through.

2 Meanwhile, bring the remaining 1½ cups water to boiling. Remove from heat; add couscous. Cover and let stand for 5 minutes. Serve bean mixture over couscous.

Nutrition Facts per serving: 527 cal., 1 g total fat (0 g sat. fat), 0 mg chol., 752 mg sodium, 115 g carb., 15 g dietary fiber, 17 g protein. **Daily Values:** 94 % vit. A, 45 % vit. C, 9 % calcium, 16 % iron.

RED BEANS AND COUSCOUS

Start to Finish: 20 minutes | Oven: 350°F | Makes: 4 servings

¾ cup walnuts, coarsely chopped
2 cups packaged julienne or shredded fresh carrot
2 cups water
1 15- to 16-ounce can red beans, rinsed and drained
1½ cups quick-cooking couscous
1½ cups refrigerated salsa
Salt

1 Preheat oven to 350°F. Place walnuts in a shallow baking pan. Bake about 8 minutes or until toasted.

2 Meanwhile, in a large saucepan combine carrot, water, and drained beans; bring to boiling. Stir in couscous. Remove from heat and let stand for 5 minutes. Stir in salsa and walnuts. Season to taste with salt.

Nutrition Facts per serving: 796 cal., 16 g total fat (2 g sat. fat), 0 mg chol., 955 mg sodium, 139 g carb., 17 g dietary fiber, 30 g protein. **Daily Values:** 210 % vit. A, 10 % vit. C, 13 % calcium, 22 % iron.

VEGETABLE CURRY

Start to Finish: 18 minutes | Makes: 4 servings

1 16-ounce package frozen baby lima beans
½ cup water
1 15-ounce can tomato sauce with garlic and onion
1½ teaspoons curry powder
2 8.8-ounce pouches cooked Spanish-style rice
¼ cup sliced green onion or snipped fresh cilantro
Olive oil (optional)

1 In medium saucepan combine lima beans and the water. Bring to boiling; reduce heat. Simmer, covered, for 5 minutes. Stir in tomato sauce and curry powder; return to boiling. Reduce heat; simmer, covered, for 3 minutes.

2 Meanwhile, heat rice according to package directions. Divide rice among 4 dinner plates; spoon bean mixture alongside rice. Garnish with green onion. If desired, drizzle with olive oil.

Nutrition Facts per serving: 385 cal., 3 g total fat (0 g sat. fat), 0 mg chol., 939 mg sodium, 72 g carb., 9 g dietary fiber, 14 g protein. **Daily Values:** 14 % vit. A, 27 % vit. C, 8 % calcium, 24 % iron.

SKILLET VEGETABLES ON CHEESE TOAST

Start to Finish: 20 minutes | Makes: 4 servings

8 slices rustic wheat bread

2 tablespoons olive oil

½ of an 8-ounce package peeled fresh baby carrots, halved lengthwise

1 8-ounce package button mushrooms, halved

1 small red onion, cut into thin wedges

4 cloves garlic, peeled and coarsely chopped

2 tablespoons water

Salt and ground black pepper

4 ounces soft goat cheese (chèvre)

Olive oil (optional)

Fresh basil (optional)

1 Preheat broiler. Place bread on baking sheet; set aside.

2 In a large skillet heat the 2 tablespoons olive oil over medium-high heat. Add carrots, mushrooms, onion, and garlic; cook for 2 to 3 minutes or just until vegetables begin to brown. Add the water; cook, covered, over medium heat about 5 minutes or until vegetables are crisp-tender, stirring once. Sprinkle with salt and pepper.

3 Meanwhile, for cheese toast, lightly toast bread in broiler 3 inches from heat for 1 to 2 minutes. Spread goat cheese on one side of each slice. Broil for 1 to 2 minutes or until cheese softens.

4 Place cheese toasts on plates; top with vegetables. If desired, drizzle with additional olive oil and sprinkle with fresh basil.

Nutrition Facts per serving: 461 cal., 21 g total fat (6 g sat. fat), 13 mg chol., 596 mg sodium, 56 g carb., 8 g dietary fiber, 15 g protein. **Daily Values:** 84 % vit. A, 8 % vit. C, 9 % calcium, 23 % iron.

SAUCY BEANS AND EGGPLANT

Start to Finish: 20 minutes | Makes: 4 servings

1 small eggplant (about 10 to 12 ounces), cut into 8 slices

3 tablespoons olive oil

Salt and freshly ground black pepper

¼ cup seasoned fine dry breadcrumbs

1 cup instant brown rice

¼ cup sliced green onion (optional)

1 15-ounce can navy or Great Northern beans, rinsed and drained

1 26-ounce jar roasted garlic pasta sauce

Crumbled feta cheese (optional)

1 Brush eggplant slices lightly with some of the olive oil. Sprinkle eggplant with salt and pepper. Coat in breadcrumbs. In a very large skillet heat the remaining olive oil over medium-high heat. Add eggplant in a single layer; cook about 5 minutes per side or until brown and tender, turning often to brown evenly.

2 Meanwhile, in a medium saucepan cook rice according to package directions. If desired, stir in green onion. For saucy beans, in another saucepan combine beans and pasta sauce; heat through.

3 Arrange eggplant slices on plates with rice and saucy beans. If desired, sprinkle with cheese and additional freshly ground black pepper.

Nutrition Facts per serving: 511 cal., 14 g total fat (2 g sat. fat), 0 mg chol., 1099 mg sodium, 82 g carb., 13 g dietary fiber, 17 g protein. **Daily Values:** 15 % vit. A, 20 % vit. C, 16 % calcium, 30 % iron.

SAUCY MUSHROOM BORSCHT

Start to Finish: 20 minutes | Makes: 4 servings

6 ounces dried medium noodles

2 tablespoons butter or margarine

1 pound assorted sliced mushrooms (about 8 cups)

3 roma tomatoes, chopped

1 8-ounce package steamed and peeled baby red beets, coarsely chopped

2½ cups beef broth

2 tablespoons cornstarch

¼ teaspoon ground black pepper
   Dairy sour cream (optional)

1 Cook noodles according to package directions; drain and keep warm.

2 Meanwhile, in a very large skillet melt butter over medium heat. Add mushrooms; cook until tender. Add tomato and beets; cook and stir for 2 minutes.

3 In a small bowl stir together ½ cup of the broth, the cornstarch, and pepper. Stir cornstarch mixture into mushroom mixture in skillet. Add remaining broth. Cook and stir until thickened and bubbly; cook and stir for 2 minutes more.

4 Serve over noodles. If desired, top with sour cream.

Nutrition Facts per serving: 303 cal., 9 g total fat (4 g sat. fat), 51 mg chol., 634 mg sodium, 47 g carb., 5 g dietary fiber, 12 g protein. **Daily Values:** 19 % vit. A, 24 % vit. C, 5 % calcium, 14 % iron.

ASIAN-STYLE BEANS AND GREENS

Start to Finish: 20 minutes | Makes: 4 servings

2 cups frozen sweet soybeans (edamame)

6 cups packaged romaine blend mixed salad greens

1 small cucumber, thinly sliced

½ cup bottled Chinese chicken salad dressing or Asian-style salad dressing

1 11-ounce can mandarin orange sections, drained

1 Cook soybeans according to package directions; drain in colander. Rinse under cold water to cool; drain.

2 In a large bowl combine the soybeans, salad greens, and cucumber. Add dressing; toss to coat. Gently stir in drained orange sections.

Nutrition Facts per serving: 191 cal., 3 g total fat (0 g sat. fat), 0 mg chol., 1020 mg sodium, 34 g carb., 5 g dietary fiber, 9 g protein. **Daily Values:** 29 % vit. A, 46 % vit. C, 16 % calcium, 12 % iron.

RAREBIT ON FOCACCIA

Start to Finish: 20 minutes | Makes: 4 sandwiches

4 6-inch Italian flatbreads (focaccia)
2 large tomatoes, sliced
   Salt and ground black pepper
1 8-ounce round Camembert cheese, chilled
⅓ cup chopped walnuts
2 tablespoons snipped fresh chives

1 Preheat broiler. Place bread on the unheated rack of a broiler pan. Top with tomato slices. Sprinkle with salt and pepper. Cut cheese into thin slices; place cheese slices on top of tomato slices.

2 Broil 4 to 5 inches from heat for 2 minutes or until cheese begins to melt. Sprinkle with walnuts; broil for 1 minute more. Sprinkle with chives.

Nutrition Facts per sandwich: 449 cal., 24 g total fat (11 g sat. fat), 41 mg chol., 1027 mg sodium, 41 g carb., 6 g dietary fiber, 21 g protein. **Daily Values:** 24 % vit. A, 19 % vit. C, 28 % calcium, 8 % iron.

PITA, CHEESE, AND VEGGIE GRILL

Start to Finish: 20 minutes | Makes: 4 servings

1 8-ounce block feta cheese, quartered
1 medium zucchini, halved lengthwise
1 medium red onion, cut into ½-inch slices
4 tablespoons bottled Italian salad dressing
  Salt and ground black pepper
4 pita bread rounds
2 medium tomatoes, cut into wedges
1 tablespoon honey

1 Drizzle cheese, zucchini, and onion slices with 2 tablespoons of the salad dressing. Sprinkle with salt and pepper.

2 For a charcoal grill, place zucchini, onion, and a 6-inch cast-iron skillet (to heat for softening the cheese) directly over medium coals. Grill zucchini and onion for 8 minutes or until tender, turning once halfway through grilling. Remove vegetables. Grill pita bread and tomato wedges on grill rack for 2 minutes or until bread is toasted and tomato is lightly charred. Place cheese in hot skillet; heat for 1 to 2 minutes to soften. (For a gas grill, preheat grill. Reduce heat to medium. Place zucchini, onion, and a 6-inch cast-iron skillet on grill rack over heat. Cover; grill as above, adding pita bread, tomato wedges, and cheese as directed.)

3 To serve, cut zucchini into chunks. Drizzle zucchini, onion, tomato, pita bread, and cheese with honey and the remaining 2 tablespoons salad dressing.

Nutrition Facts per serving: 404 cal., 17 g total fat (9 g sat. fat), 50 mg chol., 1352 mg sodium, 48 g carb., 3 g dietary fiber, 15 g protein. **Daily Values:** 17 % vit. A, 30 % vit. C, 35 % calcium, 14 % iron.

NUTTY HUMMUS OPEN-FACED SANDWICHES

Start to Finish: 15 minutes | Makes: 4 sandwiches

1 tablespoon olive oil
½ cup coarsely chopped walnuts
¾ cup coarsely chopped bottled roasted red sweet peppers
½ of a 7- to 8-ounce container roasted or zesty garlic hummus
4 ½-inch slices round country Italian bread, toasted
1 small cucumber (8 ounces), thinly sliced

1 In a large skillet heat olive oil over medium heat. Add walnuts; cook until toasted. Stir in roasted pepper; cook and stir until heated through; set aside.

2 Spread hummus on toasted bread slices; arrange on serving plates. Top with cucumber slices and walnut mixture.

Nutrition Facts per sandwich: 264 cal., 17 g total fat (2 g sat. fat), 0 mg chol., 343 mg sodium, 25 g carb., 4 g dietary fiber, 7 g protein. **Daily Values:** 1 % vit. A, 130 % vit. C, 5 % calcium, 12 % iron.

ONION-SAUCED PATTIES

Start to Finish: 20 minutes | **Makes:** 4 sandwiches

2 tablespoons olive oil

1 large sweet onion, halved and thinly sliced (about 3 cups)

1 10-ounce package refrigerated or frozen meatless burger patties

2 tablespoons mayonnaise or salad dressing

1 teaspoon yellow mustard

4 ½-inch slices ciabatta, toasted

1 cup fresh baby spinach

2 tablespoons steak sauce

1 In a large skillet heat olive oil over medium-high heat. Add onion; cook for 8 to 10 minutes or until very tender, stirring frequently.

2 Meanwhile, prepare patties according to package microwave directions.

3 In a small bowl combine mayonnaise and mustard; spread on one side of each bread slice. Place bread slices on 4 plates. Top with spinach and a burger patty. Stir steak sauce into cooked onion. Spoon onion mixture over patties.

Nutrition Facts per sandwich: 329 cal., 20 g total fat (3 g sat. fat), 3 mg chol., 688 mg sodium, 21 g carb., 5 g dietary fiber, 18 g protein. **Daily Values:** 16 % vit. A, 10 % vit. C, 6 % calcium, 15 % iron.

ZUCCHINI CAKES WITH MUSHROOM RAGOUT

Start to Finish: 20 minutes | **Oven:** 400°F | **Makes:** 4 servings

Nonstick cooking spray

1 egg, lightly beaten

½ of a medium zucchini, shredded (1 cup)

1 8.5-ounce package corn muffin mix

1 cup shredded cheddar cheese (4 ounces)

¼ cup milk

¼ teaspoon cayenne pepper

1 tablespoon olive oil

12 ounces assorted mushrooms, quartered (4 ½ cups)

Salt and ground black pepper

1 cup drained bottled roasted red sweet peppers

1 Preheat oven to 400°F. Lightly coat twelve 2½-inch muffin cups with cooking spray; set aside.

2 In a medium bowl combine egg, zucchini, muffin mix, cheese, milk, and cayenne pepper; spoon evenly into prepared muffin cups. Bake for 11 to 14 minutes or until golden.

3 Meanwhile, for mushroom ragout, in a large skillet heat olive oil over medium-high heat. Add mushrooms; cook for 3 to 4 minutes or until tender, stirring occasionally. Season with salt and black pepper. Place roasted peppers in blender; cover and blend until nearly smooth.

4 For each serving, arrange 3 zucchini cakes on a plate with some of the mushroom ragout and the pureed roasted peppers.

Nutrition Facts per serving: 443 cal., 21 g total fat (7 g sat. fat), 84 mg chol., 701 mg sodium, 49 g carb., 2 g dietary fiber, 16 g protein. **Daily Values:** 9 % vit. A, 180 % vit. C, 24 % calcium, 15 % iron.

CHAPTER 5

ONE-PAN MEALS

CHICKEN AND LEMON-BROCCOLI ALFREDO

Start to Finish: 20 minutes | **Makes:** 4 servings

4 small skinless, boneless chicken breast halves (about 1 pound)
Salt and ground black pepper
1 tablespoon olive or vegetable oil
8 ounces fresh mushrooms, halved
1 lemon
3 cups fresh broccoli florets
1 10-ounce container refrigerated light Alfredo pasta sauce

1 Sprinkle chicken lightly with salt and pepper. In a large skillet heat oil over medium heat. Add chicken and mushrooms to skillet; cook for 4 minutes, turning chicken once.

2 Meanwhile, shred 2 teaspoons lemon peel; set aside. Slice lemon. Add lemon slices and broccoli to skillet; cook, covered, about 8 minutes or until chicken is no longer pink (170°F).

3 Place chicken and vegetables on plates. Add Alfredo sauce to skillet; heat through. Serve with chicken. Sprinkle with lemon peel and pepper.

Nutrition Facts per serving: 295 cal., 12 g total fat (5 g sat. fat), 91 mg chol., 705 mg sodium, 16 g carb., 4 g dietary fiber, 35 g protein. **Daily Values:** 12 % vit. A, 140 % vit. C, 19 % calcium, 10 % iron.

CHICKEN WITH QUICK CORNBREAD DUMPLINGS

Start to Finish: 20 minutes | **Oven:** 450°F | **Makes:** 4 servings

½ cup all-purpose flour
½ teaspoon ground dried sage
¼ teaspoon salt
¼ teaspoon ground black pepper
12 ounces skinless, boneless chicken breast halves
2 tablespoons vegetable oil
2 cups frozen mixed vegetables
1 14-ounce can reduced-sodium chicken broth
½ cup milk
1 11.5-ounce package (8) refrigerated cornbread twists
½ cup finely shredded Mexican cheese blend

1 Preheat oven to 450°F. In a large self-sealing plastic bag combine flour, sage, salt, and pepper. Cut chicken into bite-size pieces. Add chicken to bag; seal bag and shake to coat. Set chicken and any remaining flour mixture aside.

2 In a large skillet heat oil over medium-high heat. Add chicken; sprinkle any remaining flour mixture over chicken. Brown chicken for 2 minutes, stirring to brown evenly (chicken will not be completely cooked). Meanwhile, place vegetables in a sieve or colander. Run cold water over vegetables to thaw. Add vegetables, broth, and milk to skillet; bring to boiling, stirring once.

3 Meanwhile, open package of cornbread twists and separate into 16 pieces.

4 Divide chicken mixture among four 16-ounce au gratin dishes or individual casseroles. Arrange cornbread pieces on top. Sprinkle with cheese. Bake for 9 to 10 minutes or until cornbread is brown.

Nutrition Facts per serving: 612 cal., 25 g total fat (7 g sat. fat), 64 mg chol., 1259 mg sodium, 60 g carb., 3 g dietary fiber, 34 g protein. **Daily Values:** 78 % vit. A, 14 % vit. C, 17 % calcium, 20 % iron.

CHICKEN AND LEMON-BROCCOLI ALFREDO

CHICKEN TORTELLINI TOSS

Start to Finish: 20 minutes | Makes: 4 servings

2 9-ounce packages refrigerated cheese tortellini

4 cups broccoli and/or cauliflower florets

1 14.5-ounce can diced tomatoes with Italian herbs, undrained

1 9-ounce package frozen roasted or grilled chicken breast strips, thawed

½ of a 10-ounce jar dried tomato pesto (½ cup)

Shaved Parmesan cheese (optional)

1 In a 4-quart Dutch oven cook tortellini according to package directions, adding the broccoli the last 3 minutes of cooking. Drain tortellini and broccoli; return to pan.

2 Stir undrained tomatoes, chicken, and pesto into tortellini mixture in pan; cook, stirring occasionally, just until heated through. If desired, garnish with Parmesan cheese.

Nutrition Facts per serving: 468 cal., 10 g total fat (4 g sat. fat), 81 mg chol., 1372 mg sodium, 61 g carb., 5 g dietary fiber, 33 g protein. **Daily Values:** 28 % vit. A, 169 % vit. C, 32 % calcium, 20 % iron.

SOUR CREAM–SAUCED CHICKEN AND APPLES

Start to Finish: 20 minutes | Makes: 4 servings

4 small skinless, boneless chicken breast halves (about 1 pound)

Salt and ground black pepper

2 tablespoons vegetable oil

2 medium red and/or green apples, sliced

2 leeks, thinly sliced

2 tablespoons snipped fresh sage

½ cup dairy sour cream

2 to 4 tablespoons milk

1 Sprinkle chicken lightly with salt and pepper. In a very large skillet heat oil over medium heat. Add chicken; cook for 10 to 12 minutes or until chicken is no longer pink (170°F), turning once. Transfer chicken to platter; cover and keep warm.

2 Add apples, leeks, and sage to skillet; cook and stir for 3 to 5 minutes or until leeks are tender. Remove from heat; stir in sour cream and enough milk to make desired consistency. Season to taste with salt and pepper. Spoon apple mixture over chicken.

Nutrition Facts per serving: 304 cal., 14 g total fat (4 g sat. fat), 77 mg chol., 246 mg sodium, 17 g carb., 3 g dietary fiber, 30 g protein. **Daily Values:** 23 % vit. A, 21 % vit. C, 8 % calcium, 11 % iron.

CHICKEN WITH STONE FRUIT SAUCE

Start to Finish: 20 minutes | Makes: 4 servings

- 4 **medium skinless, boneless chicken breast halves**
  Salt and ground black pepper
  Ground cinnamon
- 1 **tablespoon olive oil**
- 2 **nectarines, halved, pitted, and cut into wedges**
- 2 **plums, halved, pitted, and cut into wedges**
- 4 **green onions, cut into 1-inch lengths**
- ⅓ **cup apple jelly**
- 2 **tablespoons cider vinegar**

1 Sprinkle chicken lightly with salt, pepper, and cinnamon. In a large skillet heat oil over medium heat. Add chicken; cook for 10 to 12 minutes or until no pink remains (170°F), turning to brown evenly. Transfer to serving platter; cover and keep warm.

2 Add nectarines, plums, green onions, jelly, and vinegar to skillet; cook for 1 to 2 minutes or until jelly is melted and fruit softens. Spoon over chicken.

Nutrition Facts per serving: 312 cal., 5 g total fat (1 g sat. fat), 82 mg chol., 249 mg sodium, 32 g carb., 2 g dietary fiber, 34 g protein. **Daily Values:** 10 % vit. A, 19 % vit. C, 4 % calcium, 9 % iron.

TIP: If fresh fruit is not in season, substitute one 16-ounce package frozen peach slices for the nectarines and plums. Thaw the peaches in a microwave-safe bowl in the microwave on 100% power (high) about 3 minutes; drain.

CHICKEN WITH CHERRY-GINGER CHUTNEY

Start to Finish: 20 minutes | Makes: 4 servings

- 4 **medium skinless, boneless chicken breast halves, each cut into 4 pieces**
  Salt and ground black pepper
- ½ **teaspoon ground ginger**
- 1 **tablespoon olive or vegetable oil**
- 1 **large apple, thinly sliced horizontally, seeds removed**
- ½ **cup dried tart red cherries**
- ⅓ **cup coarsely chopped walnuts**
- ¼ **cup water**
- 3 **tablespoons cider vinegar**
- 4 **teaspoons packed brown sugar**

1 Sprinkle chicken lightly with salt, pepper, and ¼ teaspoon of the ginger.

2 In a large skillet heat oil over medium heat. Add chicken; cook about 12 minutes or until chicken is no longer pink (170°F), turning to brown evenly. Transfer chicken to a serving platter; cover and keep warm.

3 Add apple, cherries, and walnuts to skillet; cook for 2 minutes, stirring frequently. In a small bowl stir together water, vinegar, brown sugar, and the remaining ¼ teaspoon ginger. Add to skillet. Cook and stir for 1 minute. Serve with chicken.

Nutrition Facts per serving: 364 cal., 11 g total fat (2 g sat. fat), 82 mg chol., 248 mg sodium, 30 g carb., 3 g dietary fiber, 35 g protein. **Daily Values:** 6 % vit. A, 7 % vit. C, 5 % calcium, 10 % iron.

CHICKEN WITH CHERRY-GINGER CHUTNEY

CHICKEN WITH CAPERS

Start to Finish: 20 minutes | Makes: 4 servings

- 4 medium skinless, boneless chicken breast halves (about 1½ pounds)
- 1 tablespoon Dijon-style mustard
  Salt and ground black pepper
- ¼ cup seasoned fine dry breadcrumbs
- 4 tablespoons olive oil
- 2 small lemons
- 8 ounces haricot verts, trimmed if desired, or green beans, trimmed and halved lengthwise*
- 1 tablespoon capers
  Hot buttered pasta (optional)

1 Place 1 chicken breast half between 2 sheets of plastic wrap. Lightly pound with the flat side of a meat mallet to an even thickness; remove and discard plastic wrap. Repeat with remaining chicken breast halves. Brush chicken lightly with mustard, sprinkle evenly with salt and pepper. Place chicken on a waxed paper–lined baking sheet. Sprinkle chicken with breadcrumbs to coat.

2 In a very large skillet heat 2 tablespoons of the olive oil over medium heat. Add chicken; cook about 4 minutes per side or until no pink remains. Meanwhile, slice 1 of the lemons. Transfer chicken to serving plates.

3 Add remaining 2 tablespoons olive oil to skillet. Add beans; cook for 4 to 5 minutes or until crisp-tender, adding the lemon slices the last minute of cooking. Remove to plates with slotted spoon. Juice remaining lemon. Add lemon juice and capers to skillet; cook for 30 seconds. Drizzle over chicken and beans. If desired, serve with pasta.

Nutrition Facts per serving: 362 cal., 16 g total fat (3 g sat. fat), 99 mg chol., 546 mg sodium, 13 g carb., 4 g dietary fiber, 42 g protein. **Daily Values:** 8 % vit. A, 64 % vit. C, 7 % calcium, 14 % iron.

CHICKEN AND RICE SCRAMBLE

Start to Finish: 20 minutes | Makes: 4 servings

- 1 8.8-ounce pouch cooked Spanish-style rice
- 2 tablespoons olive oil
- 1 medium zucchini or yellow summer squash, halved lengthwise and sliced
- 2 cups cubed cooked chicken
- 8 eggs, lightly beaten
- ½ cup milk
- ¼ teaspoon salt
- ¼ teaspoon ground black pepper
- ½ cup finely shredded Mexican cheese blend (2 ounces)

1 Preheat broiler. Microwave rice according to package directions. Meanwhile, in a large broiler-proof skillet heat olive oil over medium heat. Add zucchini; cook and stir for 2 minutes. Stir in chicken and rice.

2 In a large bowl combine eggs, milk, salt, and pepper; pour over chicken mixture in skillet. Cook, without stirring, until mixture begins to set on the bottom and around the edges. Using a large spatula, lift and fold partially cooked eggs so that the uncooked portion flows underneath. Continue cooking over medium heat for 2 to 3 minutes or until egg mixture is cooked through but is still glossy and moist. Remove from heat. Sprinkle with cheese.

3 Broil 4 to 5 inches from heat for 1 to 2 minutes or until cheese melts.

Nutrition Facts per serving: 512 cal., 28 g total fat (9 g sat. fat), 500 mg chol., 667 mg sodium, 22 g carb., 1 g dietary fiber, 39 g protein. **Daily Values:** 17 % vit. A, 15 % vit. C, 22 % calcium, 19 % iron.

TURKEY SPINACH TOSS

Start to Finish: 20 minutes | Makes: 4 servings

- 2 8-ounce turkey breast tenderloins, halved horizontally
- ¼ teaspoon coarsely ground black pepper
- 2 tablespoons butter or margarine
- 2 ounces thinly sliced deli ham
- ½ cup orange juice
- 2 9- to 10-ounce packages fresh spinach
- 1 orange, cut into wedges
  Salt and coarsely ground black pepper

1 Sprinkle turkey with the ¼ teaspoon pepper. In a very large skillet melt butter over medium-high heat. Add turkey; cook about 12 minutes or until no pink remains (170°F), turning once. Meanwhile, cut ham into bite-size strips.

2 Remove turkey from skillet; cut into strips. Cover and keep warm. Add ham to hot skillet; cook and stir for 1 to 2 minutes or until ham is heated through and starting to crisp. Using a slotted spoon, remove ham from skillet. Add orange juice to skillet; bring to boiling.

3 Add spinach, half at a time, to skillet; cook about 1 minute or just until wilted, adding orange wedges with second batch of spinach. Using tongs, divide spinach mixture among 4 plates. Sprinkle with salt and pepper. Top with sliced turkey and ham. Drizzle with remaining juices from skillet.

Nutrition Facts per serving: 244 cal., 8 g total fat (4 g sat. fat), 94 mg chol., 528 mg sodium, 9 g carb., 3 g dietary fiber, 34 g protein. **Daily Values:** 244 % vit. A, 87 % vit. C, 15 % calcium, 28 % iron.

SAUCY MEATBALL SKILLET

Start to Finish: 18 minutes | Oven: 450°F | Makes: 4 servings

- 1 16-ounce tube refrigerated polenta with dried tomatoes
- 2 tablespoons olive oil
- 1 16-ounce package frozen cooked Italian-style meatballs
- 1 10-ounce container refrigerated light Alfredo pasta sauce
- 2 medium zucchini, halved lengthwise and sliced
- ¼ cup finely shredded Parmesan cheese (1 ounce)

1 Preheat oven to 450°F. Cut polenta into 12 slices. Brush both sides of each slice with olive oil and place on a baking sheet. Bake for 10 to 12 minutes or until light brown.

2 Meanwhile, in a large skillet combine meatballs, Alfredo sauce, and zucchini; cover and cook over medium heat for 10 minutes, stirring occasionally.

3 Divide polenta among 4 plates; top with meatball mixture. Sprinkle with Parmesan cheese.

Nutrition Facts per serving: 613 cal., 40 g total fat (18 g sat. fat), 102 mg chol., 1733 mg sodium, 34 g carb., 6 g dietary fiber, 29 g protein. **Daily Values:** 14 % vit. A, 41 % vit. C, 26 % calcium, 18 % iron.

CRANBERRY MEATBALL SKILLET

Start to Finish: 20 minutes | Makes: 4 servings

- 1 16-ounce can whole cranberry sauce
- 1/3 cup water
- 2 tablespoons cider vinegar
- 1 12-ounce package frozen cooked Swedish-style meatballs
- 1 cup peeled fresh baby carrots
- 8 ounces tiny new potatoes, halved
  Salt and ground black pepper

In a large skillet stir together cranberry sauce, water, and vinegar. Add meatballs, carrots, and potatoes. Bring to boiling; reduce heat. Simmer, covered, for 12 to 15 minutes or until potatoes are tender. Season to taste with salt and pepper.

Nutrition Facts per serving: 492 cal., 22 g total fat (9 g sat. fat), 30 mg chol., 857 mg sodium, 62 g carb., 5 g dietary fiber, 12 g protein. **Daily Values:** 102 % vit. A, 11 % vit. C, 6 % calcium, 7 % iron.

MEATBALLS WITH MUSTARD AND MUSHROOM SAUCE

Start to Finish: 20 minutes | Makes: 4 servings

2 tablespoons olive oil

2 cups packaged sliced fresh mushrooms

1 tablespoon Dijon-style mustard

2 tablespoons all-purpose flour

1 14-ounce can beef broth

1 16-ounce package frozen cooked Italian-style meatballs

2 cups packaged refrigerated diced potatoes

1½ cups cherry tomatoes, halved

2 tablespoons snipped fresh parsley (optional)

1 In a large skillet heat olive oil over medium heat. Add mushrooms; cook until tender. Stir in mustard and flour; gradually stir in beef broth. Bring to boiling. Stir in meatballs and potatoes; reduce heat. Simmer, covered, for 10 minutes, stirring occasionally.

2 Add tomatoes; cook just until heated through. If desired, garnish with parsley.

Nutrition Facts per serving: 510 cal., 33 g total fat (13 g sat. fat), 73 mg chol., 1341 mg sodium, 30 g carb., 6 g dietary fiber, 25 g protein. **Daily Values:** 11 % vit. A, 24 % vit. C, 6 % calcium, 17 % iron.

SUMMER STEW

Start to Finish: 20 minutes | **Makes:** 4 servings

1 **17-ounce package refrigerated cooked beef roast au jus**

1 **8-ounce package peeled fresh baby carrots, sliced**

3½ **cups water**

½ **of a 16-ounce package refrigerated rosemary and roasted garlic diced potatoes (about 2 cups)**

1 **14.5-ounce can diced fire-roasted tomatoes with garlic, undrained**

2 **tablespoons snipped fresh oregano**

Salt and freshly ground black pepper

1 Pour juices from beef roast into a large saucepan; set meat aside. Add carrots and 1 cup of the water to the saucepan. Bring to boiling; reduce heat. Simmer, covered, for 3 minutes. Add the remaining 2½ cups water, the potatoes, undrained tomatoes, and 1 tablespoon of the oregano. Return to boiling. Simmer, covered, about 3 minutes more or until vegetables are tender. Break meat into bite-size pieces and add to stew; heat through. Season with salt.

2 Spoon stew into 4 shallow bowls; top with freshly ground black pepper and the remaining 1 tablespoon oregano.

Nutrition Facts per serving: 253 cal., 9 g total fat (4 g sat. fat), 64 mg chol., 948 mg sodium, 20 g carb., 3 g dietary fiber, 25 g protein. **Daily Values:** 166 % vit. A, 52 % vit. C, 6 % calcium, 20 % iron.

ASIAN PORK SKILLET

ASIAN PORK SKILLET

Start to Finish: 18 minutes | Makes: 4 servings

2 tablespoons vegetable oil

12 ounces boneless pork, cut into bite-size strips

1½ cups water

1 3-ounce package oriental- or pork-flavor ramen noodles, broken

2 tablespoons hoisin sauce

2 cups fresh snow pea pods

2 red, yellow, and/or orange sweet peppers, cut into bite-size strips

Ground black pepper

1 In a large skillet heat oil over medium-high heat. Add pork; cook and stir about 2 minutes or until light brown.

2 Add the water to the skillet; bring to boiling. Add noodles, seasoning packet, hoisin sauce, pea pods, and sweet peppers. Return to boiling; reduce heat. Simmer, covered, for 5 minutes. Season to taste with black pepper.

Nutrition Facts per serving: 312 cal., 15 g total fat (2 g sat. fat), 54 mg chol., 646 mg sodium, 21 g carb., 2 g dietary fiber, 23 g protein. **Daily Values:** 46 % vit. A, 159 % vit. C, 4 % calcium, 13 % iron.

PORK AND HOMINY SKILLET

Start to Finish: 20 minutes | Makes: 4 servings

1 tablespoon vegetable oil

1 large sweet onion, cut into wedges

2 medium carrots, thinly sliced

1 17-ounce package refrigerated cooked pork roast au jus

2 8.8-ounce pouches cooked whole grain brown rice

1 15-ounce can yellow hominy, rinsed and drained

⅔ cup water

Ground black pepper

1 In a very large skillet heat oil over medium heat. Add onion and carrots; cook for 5 minutes.

2 Add pork with juices, breaking up meat with the back of a wooden spoon. Add rice, drained hominy, and the water; cook, covered, about 5 minutes, stirring occasionally or until heated through. Season to taste with pepper.

Nutrition Facts per serving: 503 cal., 14 g total fat (3 g sat. fat), 72 mg chol., 742 mg sodium, 63 g carb., 5 g dietary fiber, 32 g protein. **Daily Values:** 104 % vit. A, 12 % vit. C, 4 % calcium, 16 % iron.

HAM WITH CREAMED SPINACH AND SWEET POTATOES

Start to Finish: 15 minutes | Makes: 4 servings

1 22- to 24-ounce package refrigerated mashed sweet potatoes or mashed potatoes
1 9- to 10-ounce package frozen creamed spinach, thawed
2½ cups cubed cooked ham (12 ounces)
1 small red sweet pepper, chopped
¼ cup dried cranberries
Ground black pepper

1 Microwave mashed potatoes according to package directions.

2 Meanwhile, in a large saucepan combine creamed spinach, ham, sweet pepper, and cranberries; cook and stir over medium heat until heated through. Season to taste with ground black pepper.

3 Serve spinach mixture with mashed potatoes.

Nutrition Facts per serving: 368 cal., 14 g total fat (4 g sat. fat), 56 mg chol., 1357 mg sodium, 42 g carb., 5 g dietary fiber, 18 g protein. **Daily Values:** 256 % vit. A, 58 % vit. C, 13 % calcium, 14 % iron.

CUBAN FRIED RICE

Start to Finish: 20 minutes | Makes: 4 servings

1 peeled fresh pineapple, packed in juice
1 tablespoon olive oil
1 14.8-ounce pouch cooked long grain rice
2½ cups coarsely chopped cooked ham (12 ounces)
1 cup chopped or sliced red or green sweet pepper
1 jalapeño pepper, sliced (optional)
½ of a 15-ounce can black beans, rinsed and drained (¾ cup)
Lime wedges

1 Remove pineapple from container, reserving juice. Cut pineapple into ¾-inch slices; discard core if present. In a very large skillet heat olive oil over medium-high heat; add pineapple slices. Cook for 3 to 4 minutes or until pineapple begins to brown. Divide pineapple among 4 plates.

2 Meanwhile, prepare rice according to package directions. Add ham, sweet pepper, and, if desired, jalapeño pepper to skillet; cook for 3 minutes, stirring occasionally. Add beans and rice; cook about 3 minutes or until heated through, stirring occasionally. Stir in reserved pineapple juice. Serve with lime wedges.

Nutrition Facts per serving: 375 cal., 9 g total fat (1 g sat. fat), 38 mg chol., 1549 mg sodium, 58 g carb., 6 g dietary fiber, 24 g protein. **Daily Values:** 6 % vit. A, 146 % vit. C, 4 % calcium, 8 % iron.

CUBAN FRIED RICE

SAUSAGE AND POLENTA SKILLET

SAUSAGE AND POLENTA SKILLET

Start to Finish: 20 minutes | **Makes:** 4 servings

- 1 pound bulk mild Italian sausage
- 1 10-ounce container refrigerated light Alfredo pasta sauce
- 1 medium zucchini, halved lengthwise and thinly sliced
- ½ of a 16-ounce tube refrigerated cooked polenta with Italian herbs, crumbled
- ¼ cup shredded fresh basil

1 Preheat broiler. In a large broiler-proof skillet cook sausage over medium-high heat until brown. Drain sausage in a colander; carefully wipe skillet clean with paper towels.

2 Return sausage to skillet; stir in Alfredo sauce and zucchini. Bring to boiling. Sprinkle crumbled polenta over sausage mixture.

3 Broil 3 to 4 inches from the heat for 3 to 4 minutes or until heated through and light brown. Sprinkle with basil before serving.

Nutrition Facts per serving: 542 cal., 42 g total fat (17 g sat. fat), 111 mg chol., 1470 mg sodium, 18 g carb., 1 g dietary fiber, 23 g protein. **Daily Values:** 11 % vit. A, 25 % vit. C, 16 % calcium, 10 % iron.

HAM WITH LEEKS AND DILLED POTATOES

Start to Finish: 20 minutes | **Makes:** 4 servings

- 2 tablespoons vegetable oil
- 3 cups packaged refrigerated diced potatoes
- 2 medium leeks, thinly sliced
- 1½ cups cubed cooked ham (8 ounces)
- 8 ounces fresh asparagus spears, trimmed and cut into 2-inch lengths
- ⅓ cup water
  Freshly ground black pepper
- 1 cup shredded Havarti cheese with dill (4 ounces)

1 In a large skillet heat oil over medium heat. Add potatoes and leeks; cook for 5 minutes, turning mixture occasionally with a spatula. Fold in ham; cook for 2 minutes more. Add asparagus and the water; sprinkle with pepper. Cook, covered, for 3 minutes.

2 Sprinkle with cheese; cover and cook for 1 minute more.

Nutrition Facts per serving: 381 cal., 20 g total fat (1 g sat. fat), 60 mg chol., 1158 mg sodium, 33 g carb., 4 g dietary fiber, 22 g protein. **Daily Values:** 23 % vit. A, 26 % vit. C, 20 % calcium, 12 % iron.

TUNA AND TWISTY NOODLES

Start to Finish: 15 minutes | Makes: 4 servings

1 10-ounce container refrigerated light Alfredo pasta sauce

1 cup water

2 3-ounce packages ramen noodles (any flavor)

2 6-ounce cans 50% less salt chunk light tuna, drained

2 small yellow summer squash, halved lengthwise and sliced (2 cups)

1 cup sugar snap peas, halved diagonally
   Ground black pepper

In a large skillet combine Alfredo sauce and the water. Bring to boiling. Break up noodles (discard seasoning packet). Stir noodles, tuna, squash, and sugar snap peas into skillet. Return to boiling; reduce heat. Simmer, covered, for 5 minutes. Season to taste with pepper.

Nutrition Facts per serving: 396 cal., 14 g total fat (8 g sat. fat), 70 mg chol., 751 mg sodium, 35 g carb., 2 g dietary fiber, 31 g protein. **Daily Values:** 8 % vit. A, 32 % vit. C, 14 % calcium, 14 % iron.

SHRIMP QUESADILLAS

Start to Finish: 20 minutes | Makes: 4 quesadillas

4 8-inch vegetable tortillas
   Nonstick cooking spray

½ of a 7-ounce container garlic or spicy three-pepper hummus (⅓ cup)

6 ounces peeled, deveined cooked medium shrimp

1 6-ounce jar marinated artichoke hearts or half of a 16-ounce jar pickled mixed vegetables, drained and coarsely chopped

1 4-ounce package crumbled feta cheese

1 Coat 1 side of each tortilla with cooking spray. Place tortillas, sprayed side down, on work surface; spread with hummus. Top half of each tortilla with shrimp, artichoke hearts, and cheese. Fold tortillas in half, pressing gently.

2 Heat a large nonstick skillet or griddle over medium heat for 1 minute. Cook quesadillas, 2 at a time, for 4 to 6 minutes or until brown and heated through, turning once.

Nutrition Facts per quesadilla: 430 cal., 20 g total fat (7 g sat. fat), 108 mg chol., 1099 mg sodium, 42 g carb., 4 g dietary fiber, 21 g protein. **Daily Values:** 4 % vit. A, 9 % vit. C, 29 % calcium, 14 % iron.

SHRIMP QUESADILLAS

IN-A-HURRY SEAFOOD CURRY

Start to Finish: 20 minutes | Makes: 4 servings

1 tablespoon vegetable oil

1 medium sweet onion, cut into thin wedges

2 teaspoons curry powder

2 8.8-ounce pouches cooked garden vegetable–flavor rice

½ cup orange juice

1 8-ounce package flake-style imitation crabmeat

½ of a pineapple, peeled, cored, and cut into bite-size pieces

In a large skillet heat oil over medium heat. Add onion; cook just until tender. Add curry powder; cook and stir for 1 minute. Carefully stir in rice and orange juice; heat through. Add imitation crabmeat and pineapple; cook, covered, about 4 minutes or until heated through.

Nutrition Facts per serving: 331 cal., 7 g total fat (1 g sat. fat), 11 mg chol., 1141 mg sodium, 60 g carb., 2 g dietary fiber, 9 g protein. **Daily Values:** 6 % vit. A, 76 % vit. C, 6 % calcium, 17 % iron.

FISH WITH FRESH TOMATO TOPPER

Start to Finish: 18 minutes | Makes: 4 servings

½ cup fresh cilantro leaves

4 6-ounce skinless firm-textured fish fillets (such as halibut or cod), ½ to ¾ inch thick

½ teaspoon salt

½ teaspoon ground black pepper

1¼ cups water

1 cup quick-cooking couscous

2 large tomatoes, coarsely chopped

1 2.25-ounce can sliced pitted ripe olives

1 Snip half of the cilantro; set aside.

2 Place fish in a large skillet; sprinkle with the salt, pepper, and the snipped cilantro. Add the water. Bring to boiling; reduce heat. Simmer, covered, for 4 minutes. Sprinkle couscous around fish; top with tomato and olives. Cook, covered, about 5 minutes more or until fish begins to flake when tested with a fork. Sprinkle with the remaining cilantro.

Nutrition Facts per serving: 568 cal., 6 g total fat (1 g sat. fat), 54 mg chol., 539 mg sodium, 76 g carb., 6 g dietary fiber, 48 g protein. **Daily Values:** 27 % vit. A, 26 % vit. C, 13 % calcium, 19 % iron.

CHAPTER 6

NO COOK, NO BAKE

SPICY CHICKEN AND PEPPER HOAGIES

Start to Finish: 20 minutes | **Makes:** 4 sandwiches

- 4 hoagie buns
- 1/3 cup light mayonnaise or salad dressing
- 2 to 3 teaspoons finely chopped canned chipotle pepper in adobo sauce
- 1 1/4 cups packaged shredded cabbage with carrot (coleslaw mix)
- 1 small red or yellow sweet pepper, cut into matchstick-size pieces
- 1 2 1/4- to 2 1/2-pound purchased roasted chicken

1 Halve hoagie buns. Using a spoon, hollow out bun bottoms leaving a 1/2-inch shell. Discard excess bread. In a medium bowl combine mayonnaise and chipotle pepper; spread lightly in the bottom of each bread shell. Stir shredded cabbage and sweet pepper into the remaining mayonnaise mixture.

2 Remove skin and bones from chicken and discard. Coarsely chop chicken. Divide chicken among the bun shells. Top with cabbage mixture and bun tops.

Nutrition Facts per sandwich: 749 cal., 25 g total fat (6 g sat. fat), 133 mg chol., 1247 mg sodium, 77 g carb., 5 g dietary fiber, 53 g protein. **Daily Values:** 28 % vit. A, 76 % vit. C, 13 % calcium, 32 % iron.

SHRIMP AVOCADO HOAGIES

Start to Finish: 15 minutes | **Makes:** 4 sandwiches

- 1 10-to 12-ounce package frozen peeled, cooked shrimp, thawed and coarsely chopped
- 2 large avocados, halved, pitted, peeled, and chopped
- 1/2 cup purchased shredded carrot
- 1/3 cup bottled coleslaw salad dressing
- 4 hoagie buns
  Lemon wedges (optional)

1 In large bowl combine shrimp, avocado, carrot, and coleslaw dressing.

2 Halve hoagie buns. Using a spoon, slightly hollow out bun bottoms and tops leaving 1/2-inch shell. Discard excess bread. Toast buns.

3 Spoon shrimp mixture into bun shells. If desired, serve with lemon wedges.

Nutrition Facts per sandwich: 560 cal., 24 g total fat (4 g sat. fat), 144 mg chol., 825 mg sodium, 63 g carb., 8 g dietary fiber, 25 g protein. **Daily Values:** 52 % vit. A, 16 % vit. C, 13 % calcium, 26 % iron.

CRUNCHY SALMON SALAD SANDWICHES

Start to Finish: 20 minutes | **Makes:** 4 sandwiches

4 **hoagie buns**
½ **cup bottled ranch salad dressing**
2 **6-ounce cans skinless, boneless salmon, drained and flaked**
2 **small tomatoes, thinly sliced**
½ **of a medium cucumber, thinly sliced**
1 **cup shredded carrot or shredded peeled jicama (¼ of a medium)**

1 Halve hoagie buns. Spread buns with enough of the salad dressing to lightly coat. In a small bowl combine remaining salad dressing and salmon.

2 Place tomato slices on bun bottoms. Top with salmon mixture, cucumber, and carrot. Add bun tops.

Nutrition Facts per sandwich: 575 cal., 25 g total fat (4 g sat. fat), 64 mg chol., 1094 mg sodium, 57 g carb., 4 g dietary fiber, 32 g protein. **Daily Values:** 107 % vit. A, 17 % vit. C, 13 % calcium, 21 % iron.

DOUBLE DILL HAM AND SLAW SANDWICH

Start to Finish: 11 minutes | **Makes:** 4 sandwiches

- 2 cups packaged shredded cabbage with carrot (coleslaw mix)
- ¼ cup dairy sour cream dill-flavored dip
- 4 kaiser rolls, split
- 12 ounces thinly sliced cooked deli ham
- 8 thin lengthwise dill pickle slices

In a medium bowl combine shredded cabbage and dill dip; spoon onto roll bottoms. Top with ham, pickle slices, and roll tops.

Nutrition Facts per sandwich: 300 cal., 7 g total fat (3 g sat. fat), 47 mg chol., 1516 mg sodium, 35 g carb., 2 g dietary fiber, 21 g protein. **Daily Values:** 12 % vit. A, 29 % vit. C, 9 % calcium, 16 % iron.

HAM AND PINEAPPLE ROLL-UPS

Start to Finish: 15 minutes | Makes: 4 roll-ups

1 **cup packaged shredded broccoli (broccoli slaw mix)**

²/₃ **cup tub-style cream cheese spread with pineapple**

½ **cup chopped fresh pineapple**

⅛ **teaspoon ground black pepper**

4 **10-inch flour tortillas**

1 **9-ounce container thinly sliced deli-style cooked ham**

1 In a small bowl stir together shredded broccoli, ⅓ cup of the cream cheese spread, pineapple, and pepper; set aside.

2 Spread flour tortillas with the remaining ⅓ cup cream cheese spread. Divide ham evenly among the tortillas. Spoon broccoli mixture on top of the ham. Roll up; cut in half crosswise to serve.

Nutrition Facts per roll-up: 350 cal., 17 g total fat (9 g sat. fat), 61 mg chol., 1013 mg sodium, 32 g carb., 2 g dietary fiber, 16 g protein. **Daily Values:** 21 % vit. A, 52 % vit. C, 11 % calcium, 14 % iron.

CHICKEN WRAPS

Start to Finish: 14 minutes | Makes: 4 wraps

1½ **cups packaged shredded broccoli (broccoli slaw mix)**

1 **cup seedless red or green grapes, halved or quartered**

⅓ **cup bottled poppy-seed salad dressing**

1 **2¼- to 2½-pound purchased roasted chicken**

4 **10-inch flour tortillas Orange wedges (optional)**

1 In a medium bowl combine shredded broccoli, grapes, and salad dressing.

2 Remove skin and bones from chicken and discard. Slice or coarsely chop chicken. Divide chicken among the tortillas. Top with broccoli mixture. Roll up and secure with wooden toothpicks. If desired, serve with orange wedges.

Nutrition Facts per wrap: 510 cal., 28 g total fat (8 g sat. fat), 125 mg chol., 1171 mg sodium, 35 g carb., 2 g dietary fiber, 31 g protein. **Daily Values:** 21 % vit. A, 47 % vit. C, 7 % calcium, 20 % iron.

VEGGIE GARDEN WRAPS

Start to Finish: 15 minutes | Makes: 4 servings

½ cup mayonnaise or salad dressing

3 to 4 tablespoons purchased dried tomato pesto

8 to 12 6-inch corn or 7- to 8-inch flour tortillas

2 6-ounce packages refrigerated grilled chicken breast strips

2 small yellow summer squash or zucchini (8 ounces), cut into strips

1 medium green sweet pepper, cut into strips

Cilantro sprigs (optional)

1 Stir together mayonnaise and pesto; divide into 4 small bowls. Place tortillas on a microwave-safe plate; cover with paper towels. Microwave on 100% power (high) for 30 to 45 seconds or until tortillas are warm.

2 Divide chicken, squash and sweet pepper strips, and warm tortillas among 4 large shallow bowls. Place bowls of mayonnaise mixture in the shallow bowls. If desired, garnish with cilantro.

Nutrition Facts per serving: 481 cal., 30 g total fat (6 g sat. fat), 66 mg chol., 1021 mg sodium, 30 g carb., 5 g dietary fiber, 24 g protein. **Daily Values:** 6 % vit. A, 49 % vit. C, 8 % calcium, 10 % iron.

SOFT-SHELL CHICKEN TACOS

Start to Finish: 20 minutes | Makes: 4 soft-shell tacos

1 2¼- to 2½-pound purchased roasted chicken

4 7- to 8-inch flour tortillas

½ cup dairy sour cream salsa- or Mexican-flavor dip

1 large red, green, or yellow sweet pepper, cut into bite-size strips

1½ cups shredded lettuce

1 Remove skin and bones from chicken and discard. Coarsely shred 2 cups of the chicken. Reserve remaining chicken for another use.

2 Lightly spread 1 side of each tortilla with dip. Top with chicken, sweet pepper, and lettuce. Top with the remaining dip. Fold tortillas in halves to serve.

Nutrition Facts per soft-shell taco: 284 cal., 13 g total fat (5 g sat. fat), 82 mg chol., 479 mg sodium, 19 g carb., 1 g dietary fiber, 23 g protein. **Daily Values:** 25 % vit. A, 68 % vit. C, 9 % calcium, 11 % iron.

BEEF AND TAPENADE OPEN-FACE SANDWICHES

Start to Finish: 10 minutes | Makes: 4 sandwiches

⅓ cup light mayonnaise or salad dressing

1 teaspoon Dijon-style or yellow mustard

4 slices crusty country Italian or sourdough bread

¼ cup purchased olive tapenade

12 ounces thinly sliced deli roast beef

2 small tomatoes, thinly sliced

1 cup fresh baby spinach

In a small bowl combine mayonnaise and mustard. Lightly spread on 1 side of each bread slice. Spread with tapenade. Add roast beef. Top with tomato slices and spinach.

Nutrition Facts per sandwich: 362 cal., 19 g total fat (4 g sat. fat), 46 mg chol., 1681 mg sodium, 21 g carb., 2 g dietary fiber, 21 g protein. **Daily Values:** 25 % vit. A, 17 % vit. C, 6 % calcium, 15 % iron.

MEXICAN BEEF AND TORTILLAS

Start to Finish: 20 minutes | Makes 4 servings

8 6-inch corn tortillas

1 17-ounce package refrigerated beef pot roast au jus

1 14.5-ounce can diced tomatoes with green chiles, undrained

1 green sweet pepper, cut into strips

1 lime, cut into wedges

Dairy sour cream (optional)

Fresh cilantro sprigs (optional)

1 Wrap tortillas in microwave-safe paper towels. Microwave on 100% power (high) for 45 to 60 seconds or until warm. Cover; set aside.

2 Microwave beef according to package directions. Meanwhile, place undrained tomatoes in a small saucepan; heat through.

3 Remove meat, reserving juices. Cut into slices. Serve on warmed tortillas with tomatoes and green pepper strips. Drizzle with reserved juices. Pass lime wedges. If desired, serve with sour cream and cilantro.

Nutrition Facts per serving: 319 cal., 10 g total fat (5 g sat. fat), 64 mg chol., 857 mg sodium, 34 g carb., 5 g dietary fiber, 19 g protein. **Daily Values:** 15 % vit. A, 68 % vit. C, 7 % calcium, 19 % iron.

BEEF AND CUCUMBER STACKS

Start to Finish: 15 minutes | **Makes:** 4 sandwiches

- 8 slices dark rye bread
- ¼ cup mayonnaise or salad dressing
- 8 ounces thinly sliced deli roast beef
- 1 small cucumber, very thinly sliced
- ½ cup plain yogurt
- ¼ cup sliced green onion
- ½ teaspoon dried Italian seasoning
  Salt and ground black pepper

1 If desired, toast bread. Place a slice of rye bread on each of 4 plates; spread with mayonnaise. Top with beef and cucumber.

2 In a small bowl combine yogurt, green onions, and Italian seasoning; season to taste with salt and pepper. Spoon over cucumber. Top with remaining bread slices.

Nutrition Facts per sandwich: 377 cal., 15 g total fat (4 g sat. fat), 33 mg chol., 1286 mg sodium, 37 g carb., 4 g dietary fiber, 19 g protein. **Daily Values:** 3 % vit. A, 6 % vit. C, 14 % calcium, 18 % iron.

BASIL CHICKEN STACK-UPS

Start to Finish: 20 minutes | Makes: 4 servings

3 to 4 medium tomatoes
1 2¼- to 2½-pound purchased roasted chicken
1 avocado, halved, pitted, peeled, and sliced
¼ cup olive oil
1 medium lime, quartered
½ cup small fresh basil leaves
   Salt and cracked black pepper

1 Cut tomatoes into wedges and divide among 4 plates. Remove skin and bones from chicken and discard. Coarsely shred chicken into large pieces. Top tomato wedges with chicken and avocado.

2 Drizzle with olive oil. Squeeze juice from lime quarters over tomato, chicken, and avocado. Sprinkle with basil leaves, salt, and cracked pepper.

Nutrition Facts per serving: 470 cal., 31 g total fat (6 g sat. fat), 120 mg chol., 270 mg sodium, 9 g carb., 5 g dietary fiber, 41 g protein. **Daily Values:** 24 % vit. A, 21 % vit. C, 5 % calcium, 14 % iron.

CHICKEN SALAD WITH BASIL MAYONNAISE

Start to Finish: 20 minutes | Makes: 4 servings

1 2- to 2¼-pound purchased roasted chicken
¾ cup mayonnaise or salad dressing
4 tablespoons snipped fresh basil
¼ teaspoon salt
¼ teaspoon ground black pepper
1½ cups cherry or grape tomatoes, halved
1½ cups broccoli florets
6 cups shredded romaine lettuce
¼ cup finely shredded Parmesan cheese (optional)

1 Remove skin and bones from chicken and discard. Tear chicken into chunks.

2 In a large bowl combine mayonnaise, 2 tablespoons of the basil, salt, and pepper. Stir in chicken, tomatoes, and broccoli. Serve over shredded romaine. If desired, top with Parmesan cheese. Sprinkle with the remaining 2 tablespoons basil.

Nutrition Facts per serving: 763 cal., 63 g total fat (14 g sat. fat), 216 mg chol., 1709 mg sodium, 12 g carb., 4 g dietary fiber, 46 g protein. **Daily Values:** 118 % vit. A, 99 % vit. C, 6 % calcium, 24 % iron.

GREEK CHICKEN SALAD

Start to Finish: 19 minutes | Makes: 4 servings

1 5-ounce package spring mix salad greens

1 2¼- to 2½-pound purchased roasted chicken

2 small cucumbers, cut into chunks

2 medium tomatoes, cut into wedges

⅔ cup bottled Greek salad dressing with feta cheese

Cracked black pepper

Arrange greens on a serving platter. Remove skin and bones from chicken and discard. Coarsely chop chicken. Arrange chicken on the greens. Add cucumbers and tomato wedges. Drizzle with salad dressing. Sprinkle with pepper.

Nutrition Facts per serving: 473 cal., 27 g total fat (6 g sat. fat), 136 mg chol., 433 mg sodium, 9 g carb., 2 g dietary fiber, 46 g protein. **Daily Values:** 23 % vit. A, 23 % vit. C, 6 % calcium, 14 % iron.

CRUNCHY CHICKEN AND FRUIT SALAD

Start to Finish: 20 minutes | Makes: 4 servings

1 2¼- to 2½-pound purchased roasted chicken

3 oranges

⅓ cup light mayonnaise or salad dressing
  Ground black pepper

2 small red and/or green apples, cored and coarsely chopped

1 5-ounce package sweet baby lettuces

¼ cup pecan halves

1 Remove skin and bones from chicken and discard. Tear chicken into bite-size chunks; set aside.

2 For dressing, squeeze juice from 1 of the oranges. In a small bowl stir enough orange juice into mayonnaise to make dressing consistency. Season with pepper.

3 Peel and section the remaining 2 oranges. On 4 salad plates arrange lettuce, chicken, orange sections, and apples. Sprinkle with pecan halves. Pass dressing.

Nutrition Facts per serving: 455 cal., 30 g total fat (7 g sat. fat), 132 mg chol., 956 mg sodium, 23 g carb., 5 g dietary fiber, 29 g protein. **Daily Values:** 15 % vit. A, 96 % vit. C, 7 % calcium, 14 % iron.

HAWAIIAN TUNA TOSS

Start to Finish: 15 minutes | Makes: 4 servings

- 5 cups packaged shredded broccoli (broccoli slaw mix)
- 2 5-ounce pouches sweet and spicy marinated chunk light tuna
- ½ cup bottled honey Dijon salad dressing
- ½ of a small fresh pineapple, cut into 4 slices
- ½ cup macadamia nuts, chopped

1 In a large bowl toss together shredded broccoli, tuna, and salad dressing.

2 Arrange 1 pineapple slice on each of 4 plates. Spoon broccoli mixture over pineapple. Sprinkle with nuts.

Nutrition Facts per serving: 399 cal., 25 g total fat (3 g sat. fat), 31 mg chol., 480 mg sodium, 27 g carb., 5 g dietary fiber, 18 g protein. **Daily Values:** 63 % vit. A, 197 % vit. C, 7 % calcium, 11 % iron.

COOL CUCUMBER SHRIMP SLAW

Start to Finish: 10 minutes | Makes: 4 servings

- 1 12-ounce package frozen peeled, cooked shrimp, thawed and well drained
- 3 cups shredded broccoli (broccoli slaw mix)
- 1 cup grape tomatoes, halved
- ½ of an English cucumber, quartered and sliced
- ½ cup bottled cucumber ranch salad dressing
  Salt and ground black pepper
- ¼ cup dry roasted sunflower kernels (optional)

In a large bowl combine shrimp, shredded broccoli, grape tomatoes, cucumber, and salad dressing. Season to taste with salt and black pepper. If desired, sprinkle with sunflower seeds.

Nutrition Facts per serving: 255 cal., 16 g total fat (2 g sat. fat), 166 mg chol., 577 mg sodium, 9 g carb., 2 g dietary fiber, 20 g protein. **Daily Values:** 49 % vit. A, 104 % vit. C, 7 % calcium, 19 % iron.

CHAPTER 7

SANDWICHES AND PIZZA

PORTOBELLO BURGERS

Start to Finish: 20 minutes | **Makes:** 4 servings

- 4 **portobello mushrooms**
- 2 **tablespoons olive oil**
  Salt and ground black pepper
- 1 **teaspoon dried Italian seasoning, crushed**
- 4 **slices provolone cheese**
- 4 **ciabatta rolls, split**
- ¼ **cup mayonnaise or salad dressing**
- 4 **to 8 pieces bottled roasted red sweet pepper**
- ¾ **cup fresh basil leaves**

1 If desired, scrape gills from mushroom caps. Drizzle mushrooms with olive oil. Sprinkle with salt, black pepper, and Italian seasoning.

2 For a charcoal grill, grill mushrooms on the rack of uncovered grill directly over medium coals for 6 to 8 minutes or just until tender, turning once halfway through grilling. Top each mushroom with a cheese slice. Place rolls, split sides down, on grill rack. Grill about 2 minutes more or until cheese melts, mushrooms are tender, and rolls are toasted. (For a gas grill, preheat grill. Reduce heat to medium. Place mushrooms on rack over heat. Cover; grill as above, adding cheese and rolls as directed.)

3 Serve mushrooms on rolls with mayonnaise, sweet pepper pieces, and basil leaves.

Nutrition Facts per serving: 520 cal., 29 g total fat (9 g sat. fat), 25 mg chol., 972 mg sodium, 49 g carb., 4 g dietary fiber, 17 g protein. **Daily Values:** 13 % vit. A, 88 % vit. C, 31 % calcium, 22 % iron.

BARBECUE SAUCED BURGERS

Start to Finish: 20 minutes | Makes: 4 servings

- 1 **pound lean ground beef**
- 1 **to 2 tablespoons horseradish mustard**
- ¼ **teaspoon salt**
- ¼ **teaspoon ground black pepper**
- 3 **to 4 ounces white cheddar cheese or cheddar cheese, sliced**
- 4 **hamburger buns, split and toasted**
- ¼ **cup bottled barbecue sauce Arugula, tomato slices, and/or red onion slices**

1 In a large bowl combine beef, horseradish mustard, salt, and pepper; mix well. Shape into four ¾-inch-thick patties.

2 For a charcoal grill, grill patties on the rack of an uncovered grill directly over medium coals for 14 to 18 minutes or until done (160°F), turning once halfway through grilling. Top burgers with cheese during the last 1 minute of grilling. (For a gas grill, preheat grill. Reduce heat to medium. Place patties on grill rack over heat. Cover; grill as above.) Serve on buns with barbecue sauce, arugula, tomato, and/or onion.

Nutrition Facts per serving: 476 cal., 27 g total fat (12 g sat. fat), 99 mg chol., 722 mg sodium, 26 g carb., 2 g dietary fiber, 31 g protein. **Daily Values:** 10 % vit. A, 9 % vit. C, 25 % calcium, 24 % iron.

TURKEY BURGERS AND HOME FRIES

Start to Finish: 18 minutes | Makes: 4 servings

½ cup mayonnaise or salad dressing

2 teaspoons curry powder

2 tablespoons olive oil

2 cups refrigerated sliced potatoes
Salt and ground black pepper

1 pound uncooked ground turkey breast

2 ounces feta cheese with basil and tomato, crumbled

¼ teaspoon salt

4 Greek pita flatbread
Red onion slices, fresh spinach leaves, and/or crumbled feta cheese with basil and tomato

1 Preheat broiler. In a small bowl stir together mayonnaise and curry; set aside. In a very large skillet heat olive oil over medium-high heat. Add potatoes; sprinkle lightly with salt and pepper. Cook for 6 minutes; turn potatoes over. Cook 6 minutes more or until crisp.

2 In a large bowl combine turkey, 2 tablespoons of the mayonnaise mixture, the 2 ounces cheese, and the ¼ teaspoon salt. Shape into four ½-inch-thick patties.

3 Broil patties 4 inches from heat for 11 to 13 minutes or until done (165°F), turning once halfway through broiling. Spread remaining mayonnaise mixture on flatbread. Top with patties. Serve with onion, spinach, and/or additional cheese, and potatoes.

Nutrition Facts per serving: 658 cal., 33 g total fat (6 g sat. fat), 91 mg chol., 1033 mg sodium, 51 g carb., 3 g dietary fiber, 38 g protein. **Daily Values:** 4 % vit. A, 8 % vit. C, 11 % calcium, 20 % iron.

SPICY TACO TOSTADAS

Start to Finish: 15 minutes | Makes: 4 tostadas

1 18-ounce tub refrigerated taco sauce with shredded chicken

2 medium tomatoes, chopped

1 to 2 jalapeño chile peppers, seeded and chopped

5 tostada shells

3 cups packaged shredded lettuce
Shredded Mexican cheese blend (optional)

1 In a large skillet heat the taco sauce with shredded chicken, tomato, and jalapeño pepper over medium heat until heated through.

2 Place 4 of the tostada shells on a serving platter. Top with shredded lettuce. Spoon chicken mixture on top of the lettuce. Coarsely crush the remaining tostada shell; sprinkle over taco mixture. If desired, sprinkle with cheese.

Nutrition Facts per tostada: 236 cal., 8 g total fat (2 g sat. fat), 57 mg chol., 1106 mg sodium, 25 g carb., 5 g dietary fiber, 15 g protein. **Daily Values:** 24 % vit. A, 18 % vit. C, 8 % calcium, 8 % iron.

CHICKEN SANDWICHES

Start to Finish: 20 minutes | **Makes:** 4 sandwiches

8 ounces asparagus spears, trimmed
2 tablespoons olive oil
Salt and coarsely ground black pepper
4 4-inch portobello mushroom caps
4 small skinless, boneless chicken breast halves
8 ½-inch slices country Italian bread*
1 8-ounce tub cream cheese spread with chive and onion

1 Tear off a 36x18-inch piece of heavy foil; fold in half to make an 18-inch square. Place asparagus in center of foil; drizzle with 1 tablespoon of the olive oil and sprinkle lightly with salt and pepper. Bring up opposite edges of foil and seal with a double fold. Fold remaining edges to completely enclose asparagus, leaving space for steam to escape. Set aside.

2 Remove stems from mushrooms. Brush chicken and mushrooms with the remaining 1 tablespoon olive oil; sprinkle lightly with salt and pepper. For a charcoal grill, place chicken, mushrooms, and foil packet with asparagus on the rack of an uncovered grill directly over medium coals. Grill for 12 to 15 minutes or until chicken is no longer pink (170°F) and mushrooms are tender, turning chicken and mushrooms once halfway through grilling. (For a gas grill, preheat grill. Reduce heat to medium. Place chicken, mushrooms, and foil packet on grill rack over heat. Cover; grill as above.) Remove chicken, mushrooms, and foil packet from grill; slice mushrooms.

3 Toast bread slices on grill rack for 1 to 2 minutes, turning once. Spread 1 side of each slice with cream cheese. On serving plates stack half of the slices, spread sides up, chicken, remaining bread slices, mushrooms, and asparagus.

Nutrition Facts per sandwich: 583 cal., 29 g total fat (15 g sat. fat), 121 mg chol., 751 mg sodium, 40 g carb., 4 g dietary fiber, 37 g protein. **Daily Values:** 17 % vit. A, 52 % vit. C, 6 % calcium, 19 % iron.

TIP: If bread slices are too large, use halved slices of bread.

PEPPERED TURKEY PANINI

Start to Finish: 20 minutes | Makes: 4 panini

- ⅓ cup broken walnuts (optional)
- 8 ½-inch slices country Italian bread
- ½ cup refrigerated classic bruschetta topper
- 2 tablespoons mayonnaise or salad dressing
- 12 ounces sliced cooked peppered turkey breast
- 1 cup large spinach leaves
  Olive oil

1 Preheat a very large skillet over medium heat. If desired, add walnuts to skillet; cook and stir for 2 minutes or until toasted. Remove nuts from skillet; set aside.

2 To assemble sandwiches, spread 4 of the bread slices with bruschetta topper. Spread the remaining 4 slices with mayonnaise. On bruschetta slices layer walnuts (if using), turkey, and spinach. Top with remaining bread slices, mayonnaise sides down. Brush tops and bottoms of sandwiches lightly with olive oil.

3 Place the sandwiches in the hot skillet; weight with additional skillet (add food cans for more weight). Grill for 2 minutes; turn. Replace weights; cook about 2 minutes more or until golden and heated through.

Nutrition Facts per panini: 448 cal., 23 g total fat (4 g sat. fat), 43 mg chol., 1522 mg sodium, 35 g carb., 2 g dietary fiber, 26 g protein. **Daily Values:** 18 % vit. A, 4 % vit. C, 9 % calcium, 13 % iron.

BEEFY CIABATTA SANDWICHES

Start to Finish: 20 minutes | Makes: 4 sandwiches

- 8 **dried tomato slices or halves (not oil packed)**
- 12 **ounces beef sirloin steak, about ¾ inch thick**
- 1 **small red onion, thinly sliced**
- 2 **tablespoons olive oil**
  Salt and ground black pepper
- 4 **ciabatta rolls, split, or square bagels**
- ¼ **cup mayonnaise or salad dressing**
- 1 **cup packaged mixed salad greens**

1 Preheat broiler. Place tomatoes in a small microwave-safe bowl; cover with water. Microwave on 100% power (high) for 1 minute. Set aside.

2 Brush steak and onion slices with olive oil; sprinkle with salt and pepper. Arrange steak and onion on the unheated rack of a broiler pan. Broil 3 to 4 inches from heat for 12 to 16 minutes or until desired doneness, turning once. Thinly slice beef across the grain into bite-size strips.

3 Meanwhile, drain tomatoes. Spread mayonnaise on bagels; layer bagel bottom with steak, onion, tomato, and salad greens; top with bagel top.

Nutrition Facts per sandwich: 451 cal., 22 g total fat (4 g sat. fat), 51 mg chol., 681 mg sodium, 40 g carb., 3 g dietary fiber, 26 g protein. **Daily Values:** 4 % vit. A, 6 % vit. C, 8 % calcium, 25 % iron.

MEATLOAF OPEN-FACERS

Start to Finish: 18 minutes | Makes: 4 sandwiches

- 4 **½-inch slices eggplant**
- 2 **tablespoons olive oil**
  Salt and ground black pepper
- 1 **17-ounce package refrigerated meatloaf with tomato sauce**
- 4 **1-inch diagonal slices Italian bread, toasted**
- ½ **cup no-salt-added tomato sauce**
- ¼ **cup finely shredded Parmesan cheese (optional)**

1 Preheat broiler. Brush eggplant on both sides with olive oil. Sprinkle with salt and pepper. Place eggplant slices on unheated rack of broiler pan. Broil 3 to 4 inches from heat for 2 to 3 minutes per side or until brown.

2 Meanwhile, slice meatloaf. Place in a large skillet over medium-high heat. Pour the no-salt-added tomato sauce over meatloaf slices; cook about 6 minutes or until heated through.

3 Place meatloaf slices on toasted bread; top with eggplant, any remaining sauce, and, if desired, Parmesan cheese.

Nutrition Facts per sandwich: 327 cal., 16 g total fat (5 g sat. fat), 64 mg chol., 707 mg sodium, 21 g carb., 2 g dietary fiber, 27 g protein. **Daily Values:** 2 % vit. A, 7 % vit. C, 3 % calcium, 15 % iron.

MEATBALLS ON CIABATTA

Start to Finish: 15 minutes | Makes: 6 sandwiches

⅓ cup olive oil

¼ cup lemon juice

1 bunch flat-leaf parsley, large stems removed

2 cloves garlic
  Salt and ground black pepper

1 16- to 18-ounce package frozen cooked Italian-style meatballs, thawed

6 ciabatta rolls, split and toasted

½ of a small head romaine lettuce, chopped or torn

1 In a food processor or blender combine olive oil, lemon juice, parsley, and garlic; process until finely chopped. Season to taste with salt and pepper.

2 Transfer parsley mixture to a large skillet over medium heat. Add meatballs; heat through, covered, stirring and spooning sauce over meatballs occasionally.

3 Stack ciabatta halves, toasted sides up, on plates. Top with romaine. Using a slotted spoon, remove meatballs from skillet; place on romaine. Drizzle with warm parsley mixture from skillet.

Nutrition Facts per sandwich: 534 cal., 31 g total fat (10 g sat. fat), 49 mg chol., 1002 mg sodium, 43 g carb., 6 g dietary fiber, 20 g protein. **Daily Values:** 5 % vit. A, 6 % vit. C, 1 % calcium, 29 % iron.

BACON AND EGG SALAD SANDWICHES

Start to Finish: 20 minutes | **Makes:** 4 sandwiches

6 **eggs**
8 **slices applewood-smoked bacon**
8 **slices challah bread**
½ **cup mayonnaise or salad dressing**
2 **teaspoons yellow mustard**
12 **to 16 basil leaves**
½ **of an English cucumber, chopped**

1 Place eggs in a medium saucepan; cover with water. Bring to boiling over high heat; cover and remove from heat. After 6 minutes, remove 2 eggs. Rinse with cold water; peel and set aside. Let remaining eggs stand in hot water for 4 minutes more. Drain; rinse with cold water. Peel and coarsely chop the 10-minute eggs.

2 Meanwhile, in a very large skillet cook bacon until crisp; remove with a slotted spoon. Drain bacon on paper towels. Discard drippings and wipe skillet with paper towel. Lightly toast both sides of bread slices in skillet. In a small bowl combine mayonnaise and mustard.

3 Top 4 of the bread slices with basil leaves, chopped egg, and cucumber. Halve the remaining two eggs and place one half on each sandwich. Top with mayonnaise mixture, bacon, and remaining bread slices.

Nutrition Facts per sandwich: 614 cal., 40 g total fat (10 g sat. fat), 391 mg chol., 765 mg sodium, 38 g carb., 2 g dietary fiber, 22 g protein. **Daily Values:** 19 % vit. A, 3 % vit. C, 7 % calcium, 20 % iron.

PORK-VEGGIE SANDWICHES

Start to Finish: 15 minutes | Makes: 4 servings (2 pieces each)

1 18.4-ounce peppercorn-seasoned pork tenderloin
1 ripe avocado
¼ teaspoon salt
⅛ teaspoon ground black pepper
1 10-inch focaccia, cut into quarters and split horizontally
½ of a medium red onion, thinly sliced
1 large tomato, cored and sliced

1 Preheat broiler. Cut tenderloin into ½-inch slices; flatten slightly with palm of hand. Arrange slices on the unheated rack of a broiler pan. Broil 4 inches from the heat for 4 to 6 minutes or just until slightly pink in center, turning once.

2 Meanwhile, halve, seed, and peel avocado; transfer to a small bowl. Mash with a fork. Stir in salt and pepper.

3 Spread bottoms of bread quarters with avocado mixture. Layer red onion, pork, and tomato on top of avocado mixture. Add bread tops. Cut each in half to serve.

Nutrition Facts per serving: 476 cal., 14 g total fat (4 g sat. fat), 61 mg chol., 925 mg sodium, 57 g carb., 7 g dietary fiber, 35 g protein. **Daily Values:** 8 % vit. A, 19 % vit. C, 13 % calcium, 13 % iron.

CURRIED HAM AND BRIE SANDWICHES

Start to Finish: 12 minutes | Makes: 4 sandwiches

¼ cup mango chutney
2 tablespoons mayonnaise or salad dressing
½ teaspoon curry powder
8 ½-inch slices country Italian bread
⅓ cup creamy-style Brie cheese
12 ounces thinly sliced cooked ham
Leaf lettuce, sliced tomato, and/or sliced sweet onion (optional)

1 Place chutney in a small bowl; snip up any large fruit pieces. Stir in mayonnaise and curry powder; set aside.

2 Spread 4 of the bread slices with Brie cheese. Top with ham. If desired, add lettuce, tomato, and/or onion. Spread chutney mixture on the remaining bread slices; place, spread sides down, on top of sandwiches.

Nutrition Facts per sandwich: 363 cal., 18 g total fat (6 g sat. fat), 63 mg chol., 1498 mg sodium, 30 g carb., 3 g dietary fiber, 20 g protein. **Daily Values:** 4 % vit. A, 10 % vit. C, 8 % calcium, 13 % iron.

TUNA BRUSCHETTA SANDWICHES

Start to Finish: 20 minutes | **Makes:** 4 servings (2 bruschetta each)

- 8 1-inch slices country Italian bread
- 1 8-ounce package frozen spinach-artichoke dip, thawed
- 2 5-ounce pouches lemon-pepper-marinated chunk light tuna
- 2 small red and/or yellow sweet peppers, cut into thin strips
- 1 cup shredded Italian cheese blend (4 ounces)

1 Preheat broiler. Place bread on a baking sheet. Broil 4 inches from heat about 2 minutes or until toasted. Remove from oven.

2 Turn bread slices; spread with dip. Top with tuna, pepper strips, and cheese. Broil for 3 to 4 minutes or until cheese melts and mixture is heated through.

Nutrition Facts per serving: 488 cal., 15 g total fat (6 g sat. fat), 60 mg chol., 1132 mg sodium, 47 g carb., 3 g dietary fiber, 40 g protein. **Daily Values:** 43 % vit. A, 88 % vit. C, 37 % calcium, 14 % iron.

CATFISH PO' BOYS

Start to Finish: 20 minutes | **Makes:** 4 sandwiches

1 to 1¼ pounds catfish fillets
Salt and ground black pepper
½ cup fine dry breadcrumbs
2 tablespoons olive oil
4 hoagie buns, split and, if desired, toasted
2 medium red and/or yellow sweet peppers, sliced into rings
1 cup shredded Monterey Jack cheese with jalapeño peppers (4 ounces)
1 cup purchased deli coleslaw
Bottled hot pepper sauce (optional)
Small hot peppers (optional)

1 Cut fish into 3-inch pieces. Sprinkle lightly with salt and pepper. Coat fish with breadcrumbs. In a very large skillet heat olive oil over medium heat. Add fish; cook for 6 to 8 minutes or until golden brown and fish begins to flake when tested with a fork, turning once.

2 Divide fish among buns. Top with sweet pepper rings, cheese, and coleslaw. If desired, pass hot pepper sauce and serve with hot peppers.

Nutrition Facts per sandwich: 675 cal., 30 g total fat (10 g sat. fat), 86 mg chol., 1004 mg sodium, 67 g carb., 4 g dietary fiber, 35 g protein. **Daily Values:** 49 % vit. A, 144 % vit. C, 33 % calcium, 20 % iron.

VEGGIE-CHEESE SANDWICHES

Start to Finish: 20 minutes | **Makes:** 4 sandwiches

8 ½-inch slices country French white bread
4 teaspoons olive oil
2 tablespoons honey mustard
4 ounces thinly sliced cheddar cheese
½ cup thinly sliced cucumber
½ cup fresh spinach leaves
¼ cup thinly sliced red onion

1 Brush 1 side of each bread slice with olive oil; brush other side with mustard. Top the mustard sides of 4 slices with cheese, cucumber, spinach, and onion. Top with remaining bread slices, mustard sides down.

2 Preheat an indoor electric grill. Place sandwiches on grill. If using a covered grill, close lid. Grill sandwiches for 3 to 5 minutes or until bread is golden. (For an uncovered grill, allow 6 to 8 minutes, turning once halfway through grilling.) Serve immediately.

Nutrition Facts per sandwich: 194 cal., 7 g total fat (1 g sat. fat), 0 mg chol., 244 mg sodium, 22 g carb., 1 g dietary fiber, 10 g protein. **Daily Values:** 8 % vit. A, 3 % vit. C, 29 % calcium, 15 % iron.

BEEF AND BLUE CHEESE WRAPS

Start to Finish: 20 minutes | **Makes:** 4 wraps

- 3 tablespoons mayonnaise or salad dressing
- 1 teaspoon dried thyme, crushed
- 2 tablespoons yellow mustard
- 4 8-inch flour tortillas
- 12 ounces thinly sliced deli roast beef
- 1 12-ounce jar roasted red sweet peppers, drained
- ⅓ cup crumbled blue cheese
- 4 cups mixed salad greens
  Olive oil (optional)
  Crumbled blue cheese (optional)

1 In a small bowl stir together mayonnaise and dried thyme. Remove 1 tablespoon of the mayonnaise mixture; set aside. Stir mustard into the remaining mayonnaise mixture.

2 Spread one side of each tortilla with mayonnaise-mustard mixture. Evenly divide roast beef, roasted peppers, and the ⅓ cup blue cheese among the tortillas. Roll to make wraps; brush with reserved mayonnaise-thyme mixture.

3 In a very large skillet lightly brown tortilla wraps over medium heat about 2 minutes per side. Cut each wrap in half. Divide greens among 4 salad plates. If desired, drizzle greens with olive oil and sprinkle with additional blue cheese. Place halved wraps on top of greens.

Nutrition Facts per wrap: 395 cal., 23 g total fat (7 g sat. fat), 50 mg chol., 1145 mg sodium, 22 g carb., 3 g dietary fiber, 21 g protein. **Daily Values:** 12 % vit. A, 261 % vit. C, 12 % calcium, 20 % iron.

BEEF AND CABBAGE WRAPS

Start to Finish: 20 minutes | Oven: 350°F | Makes: 4 servings (2 wraps each)

8 8-inch flour tortillas
12 ounces lean ground beef
½ cup chopped onion
1 cup frozen whole kernel corn
½ to ⅔ cup bottled barbecue sauce
2 cups packaged shredded cabbage with carrot (coleslaw mix)

1 Preheat oven to 350°F. Wrap tortillas tightly in foil; place on baking sheet. Warm in oven about 10 minutes or until heated through.

2 Meanwhile, for filling, in a large skillet cook beef and onion until beef is brown and onion is tender; drain off fat. Stir in corn and ⅓ cup of the barbecue sauce; cook and stir until heated through.

3 To serve, spread tortillas with some of the remaining barbecue sauce. Spoon about ½ cup filling on each tortilla. Add shredded cabbage. Roll to make wraps.

Nutrition Facts per serving: 391 cal., 14 g total fat (4 g sat. fat), 54 mg chol., 535 mg sodium, 46 g carb., 3 g dietary fiber, 21 g protein. **Daily Values:** 12 % vit. A, 30 % vit. C, 9 % calcium, 21 % iron.

CHICKEN SATAY PIZZA

Start to Finish: 20 minutes | Oven: 425°F | Makes: 4 servings

- 1 **12-inch Italian bread shell (such as Boboli)**
- ¼ **cup bottled peanut sauce**
- 1 **6-ounce package refrigerated cooked chicken breast strips**
- ½ **cup packaged coarsely shredded fresh carrot**
- 1 **cup shredded Monterey Jack cheese (4 ounces)**
- ¼ **cup sliced green onion and/or chopped peanuts (optional)**

1 Preheat oven to 425°F. Place bread shell on a 12-inch pizza pan or large baking sheet. Spread peanut sauce over bread shell. Top with chicken and carrot. Sprinkle with cheese and, if desired, green onion and/or peanuts.

2 Bake, uncovered, for 10 to 12 minutes or until heated through.

Nutrition Facts per serving: 500 cal., 18 g total fat (6 g sat. fat), 56 mg chol., 1509 mg sodium, 56 g carb., 0 g dietary fiber, 30 g protein. **Daily Values:** 56 % vit. A, 1 % vit. C, 39 % calcium, 7 % iron.

CHICKEN SALAD PITA PIZZAS

Start to Finish: 20 minutes | Makes: 4 pizzas

- 4 **pita bread rounds**
- 4 **cups packaged torn mixed salad greens**
- 3 **tablespoons bottled reduced-calorie creamy Caesar salad dressing**
- 1 **6-ounce package refrigerated Southwest-flavor cooked chicken breast strips**
- 1 **cup shredded Italian cheese blend (4 ounces)**

1 Preheat broiler. Arrange pita bread rounds on a large baking sheet. In a large bowl toss together mixed greens and salad dressing; pile on the pita rounds. Top with chicken and cheese.

2 Broil 4 inches from heat for 1 to 1½ minutes or until cheese begins to brown and greens begin to wilt. Serve with knives and forks.

Nutrition Facts per pizza: 340 cal., 11 g total fat (5 g sat. fat), 49 mg chol., 1124 mg sodium, 37 g carb., 2 g dietary fiber, 23 g protein. **Daily Values:** 14 % vit. A, 6 % vit. C, 27 % calcium, 13 % iron.

BUFFALO CHICKEN PIZZAS

Start to Finish: 20 minutes | **Oven:** 450°F | **Makes:** 4 pizzas

4 **pita bread rounds**

¼ **cup bottled blue cheese salad dressing**

1 **9-ounce package refrigerated Southwest-flavor cooked chicken breast strips**

¾ **cup thinly sliced celery**

Blue cheese crumbles (optional)

Bottled hot pepper sauce or buffalo wing sauce (optional)

1 Preheat oven to 450°F. Place pita rounds on baking sheet. Brush with blue cheese dressing. Top with chicken strips and celery. Bake, uncovered, about 10 minutes or until heated through and pitas are crisp.

2 Transfer pitas to 4 plates. If desired, sprinkle with blue cheese and pass hot pepper sauce.

Nutrition Facts per pizza: 327 cal., 11 g total fat (2 g sat. fat), 44 mg chol., 1084 mg sodium, 36 g carb., 2 g dietary fiber, 20 g protein. **Daily Values:** 3 % vit. A, 2 % vit. C, 7 % calcium, 12 % iron.

CHORIZO-TOPPED PIZZAS

Start to Finish: 20 minutes | Makes: 4 pizzas

8 ounces chorizo sausage
1 cup deli-fresh chunky garden salsa with corn and beans
   Nonstick cooking spray
4 7- to 8-inch flour tortillas
1 cup shredded Mexican cheese blend (4 ounces)
1 avocado, halved, pitted, peeled, and sliced
½ cup chopped green onion
¼ cup snipped fresh cilantro
   Lime wedges

1 Preheat broiler. In a large skillet crumble and cook chorizo over medium heat until no pink remains; drain in colander. In a small saucepan heat salsa over medium heat until heated through.

2 Meanwhile, lightly coat a large baking sheet with cooking spray. Arrange tortillas, 2 at a time, on the baking sheet; top each with one-fourth of the cheese. Broil 3 to 4 inches from heat for 2 to 3 minutes or until cheese melts and tortillas start to brown. Top each pizza with ¼ of the warm salsa, cooked chorizo, avocado, green onion, and cilantro. Serve with lime wedges.

Nutrition Facts per pizza: 588 cal., 41 g total fat (15 g sat. fat), 75 mg chol., 1242 mg sodium, 31 g carb., 6 g dietary fiber, 24 g protein. **Daily Values:** 2 % vit. A, 22 % vit. C, 20 % calcium, 11 % iron.

TUNA ALFREDO PIZZA

Start to Finish: 20 minutes | Oven: 425°F | Makes: 4 servings

1 12-inch Italian bread shell (such as Boboli)
⅔ cup refrigerated light Alfredo pasta sauce
1 5-ounce pouch lemon-pepper-marinated chunk light tuna, flaked
1 small zucchini or yellow summer squash, thinly sliced
⅓ cup finely shredded Parmesan cheese
   Ground black pepper

1 Preheat oven to 425°F. Place bread shell on a pizza pan or a large baking sheet. Spread with Alfredo sauce. Top with tuna and zucchini; sprinkle with Parmesan cheese and black pepper.

2 Bake for 10 to 12 minutes or until heated through.

Nutrition Facts per serving: 438 cal., 12 g total fat (4 g sat. fat), 42 mg chol., 1100 mg sodium, 54 g carb., 0 g dietary fiber, 30 g protein. **Daily Values:** 3 % vit. A, 9 % vit. C, 32 % calcium, 4 % iron.

BEEF AND BLUE PIZZA

Start to Finish: 18 minutes | Oven: 425°F | Makes: 4 servings

2 tablespoons olive oil

½ of a medium red onion, cut into thin slivers

1 12-inch Italian bread shell (such as Boboli)

8 ounces thinly sliced deli roast beef

½ cup chopped sweet pepper

4 ounces blue cheese, crumbled

¼ teaspoon pizza seasoning (optional)

1 Position oven rack in the center of the oven. Preheat oven to 425°F. In a large skillet heat 1 tablespoon of the olive oil over medium-high heat. Add onion; cook for 3 to 5 minutes or just until tender.

2 Meanwhile, place bread shell on a large baking sheet; brush with the remaining 1 tablespoon olive oil. Bake for 5 minutes. Change oven setting to broil.

3 Meanwhile, lay the beef on a cutting board; layer the slices to make a stack if necessary. Slice beef crosswise into strips. Top partially baked bread shell with beef, sweet pepper, cooked onion, and blue cheese. If desired, sprinkle with pizza seasoning.

4 Broil pizza for 4 to 5 minutes or until toppings are heated through and crust is light brown. Cut into wedges to serve.

Nutrition Facts per serving: 523 cal., 20 g total fat (7 g sat. fat), 56 mg chol., 1637 mg sodium, 54 g carb., 1 g dietary fiber, 31 g protein. **Daily Values:** 23 % vit. A, 96 % vit. C, 34 % calcium, 10 % iron.

ROASTED VEGETABLE PIZZA

Start to Finish: 20 minutes | Makes: 4 servings

12 ounces asparagus spears, trimmed and cut into 2-inch lengths

1 medium yellow summer squash, halved lengthwise and thinly sliced

⅓ cup bottled Italian salad dressing

½ of a 6.3-ounce container semi-soft cheese with garlic and herbs (about ½ cup)

1 12-inch Italian bread shell (such as Boboli)

½ cup finely shredded Parmesan cheese (2 ounces)
Freshly ground black pepper

1 Preheat broiler. In a 15x10x1-inch baking pan combine asparagus, squash, and salad dressing. Broil 3 to 4 inches from heat for 6 minutes, stirring twice. Drain, reserving 2 tablespoons of the dressing. Place semi-soft cheese in a small bowl; stir in hot reserved dressing until combined.

2 Place bread shell on a baking sheet. Spread with semi-soft cheese mixture. Top with drained vegetables; sprinkle with Parmesan cheese and pepper.

3 Broil for 3 to 4 minutes or until heated through.

Nutrition Facts per serving: 458 cal., 22 g total fat (8 g sat. fat), 32 mg chol., 1037 mg sodium, 49 g carb., 3 g dietary fiber, 18 g protein. **Daily Values:** 9 % vit. A, 8 % vit. C, 26 % calcium, 18 % iron.

CHAPTER 8

SOUPS

HEARTY CHICKEN AND BARLEY SOUP

Start to Finish: 20 minutes | **Makes:** 4 servings

2 14-ounce cans chicken broth with roasted garlic
1 cup water
½ cup quick-cooking barley
1 2¼- to 2½-pound purchased roasted chicken
1 cup packaged julienne or shredded fresh carrot
1 cup fresh pea pods, halved
Ground black pepper

1 In a large saucepan combine broth, the water, and barley. Bring to boiling; reduce heat. Simmer, covered, for 10 minutes.

2 Meanwhile, remove skin and bones from chicken and discard. Coarsely shred 2 cups of the chicken. Reserve remaining chicken for another use. Stir the 2 cups chicken, carrot, and pea pods into the barley mixture; cook over medium heat until heated through. Season to taste with pepper.

Nutrition Facts per serving: 280 cal., 12 g total fat (4 g sat. fat), 77 mg chol., 1301 mg sodium, 25 g carb., 5 g dietary fiber, 21 g protein. **Daily Values:** 96 % vit. A, 24 % vit. C, 3 % calcium, 12 % iron.

TURKEY TORTILLA SOUP

Start to Finish: 20 minutes | **Makes:** 4 servings

2 tablespoons vegetable oil
3 6-inch corn tortillas, cut into strips
2 14-ounce cans reduced-sodium chicken broth
1 cup purchased red or green salsa
2 cups cubed cooked turkey (10 ounces)
1 large zucchini, coarsely chopped
  Snipped fresh cilantro (optional)
  Dairy sour cream (optional)
  Lime wedges (optional)

1 In a large skillet heat oil over medium heat. Add tortilla strips; cook until crisp. Using a slotted spoon, remove tortilla strips; drain on paper towels.

2 In a large saucepan combine broth and salsa. Bring to boiling over medium-high heat. Add turkey and zucchini; heat through. Serve in bowls; top with tortilla strips. If desired, sprinkle with cilantro and serve with sour cream and lime wedges.

Nutrition Facts per serving: 262 cal., 11 g total fat (2 g sat. fat), 53 mg chol., 920 mg sodium, 16 g carb., 3 g dietary fiber, 26 g protein. **Daily Values:** 6 % vit. A, 21 % vit. C, 6 % calcium, 11 % iron.

CURRIED TURKEY SOUP

Start to Finish: 20 minutes | **Makes:** 4 servings

1   **2-ounce turkey breast tenderloin, cut into ½-inch cubes**
2   **teaspoons curry powder**
1   **tablespoon vegetable oil**
5   **cups water**
1   **3-ounce package chicken-flavor ramen noodles**
1   **cup broccoli florets**
1   **cup packaged julienne or shredded fresh carrot**
    Salt and ground black pepper
    Fresh cilantro leaves (optional)

1 In a large bowl combine turkey and curry powder; toss to coat. In a large saucepan heat oil over medium-high heat. Add turkey; cook and stir about 2 minutes or until brown. Carefully stir in the water, seasoning packet from ramen noodles, broccoli, and carrot; cook, covered, over high heat just until boiling.

2 Break up noodles; add to soup. Cook, uncovered, for 3 minutes, stirring once or twice. Season to taste with salt and pepper. If desired, top with cilantro.

Nutrition Facts per serving: 241 cal., 8 g total fat (2 g sat. fat), 53 mg chol., 520 mg sodium, 19 g carb., 2 g dietary fiber, 24 g protein. **Daily Values:** 106 % vit. A, 37 % vit. C, 5 % calcium, 11 % iron.

SWEET SAUSAGE AND ASPARAGUS SOUP

Start to Finish: 20 minutes | **Makes:** 4 servings

2   **14-ounce cans chicken broth with roasted garlic**
2   **cups water**
1   **cup small shell macaroni**
8   **ounces frozen cooked mild Italian sausage links, thawed and thinly sliced (3 links)**
8   **ounces asparagus spears, trimmed and cut into 1-inch lengths**
    Ground black pepper
¼   **cup shredded fresh basil**

In a Dutch oven combine broth and the water; bring to boiling. Add macaroni; boil gently, uncovered, for 5 minutes. Add sausage and asparagus; boil gently, uncovered, about 5 minutes more or until macaroni is tender. Season to taste with pepper. Stir in basil just before serving.

Nutrition Facts per serving: 177 cal., 6 g total fat (2 g sat. fat), 19 mg chol., 1114 mg sodium, 19 g carb., 1 g dietary fiber, 13 g protein. **Daily Values:** 11 % vit. A, 4 % vit. C, 3 % calcium, 11 % iron.

VEGGIE FISH CHOWDER

Start to Finish: 20 minutes | Makes: 4 servings

1 **pound firm-textured white fish fillets or steaks, cut into 4 pieces**
Freshly ground black pepper
1 **tablespoon olive oil**
2 **medium carrots, thinly sliced**
1 **cup sugar snap peas, halved diagonally**
1 **14-ounce can vegetable broth**
2¼ **cups water**
1 **4-ounce package (or half a 7.2-ounce package) butter-and-herb-flavor mashed potatoes**
Salt and ground black pepper
Shaved Parmesan cheese (optional)

1 Sprinkle fish lightly with freshly ground pepper. In a 4-quart Dutch oven heat olive oil over medium-high heat. Add fish, carrots, and sugar snap peas; cook for 3 minutes.

2 Add broth and the water. Bring to boiling; reduce heat. Simmer, covered, about 3 minutes or until fish begins to flake when tested with a fork.

3 Place mashed potatoes in a small bowl. Carefully remove 1¼ cups of the hot broth from Dutch oven; stir broth into potatoes (mixture will be thick).

4 Divide mashed potato mixture among 4 bowls. Break fish into bite-size pieces. Ladle hot fish and vegetable mixture over potatoes. Season to taste with salt and pepper. If desired, serve with Parmesan cheese.

Nutrition Facts per serving: 264 cal., 7 g total fat (2 g sat. fat), 49 mg chol., 1001 mg sodium, 27 g carb., 3 g dietary fiber, 23 g protein. **Daily Values:** 108 % vit. A, 14 % vit. C, 6 % calcium, 7 % iron.

PEPPER AND BASIL TORTELLINI SOUP

Start to Finish: 20 minutes | Makes: 4 servings

1 14.5-ounce can Italian-style stewed tomatoes, undrained
1 14-ounce can reduced-sodium chicken broth
1¼ cups water
1 9-ounce package refrigerated three-cheese tortellini
2 small red and/or yellow sweet peppers, chopped
⅓ cup snipped fresh basil
  Grated Parmesan cheese (optional)

In a large saucepan combine undrained tomatoes, chicken broth, and the water; bring to boiling. Add tortellini and peppers. Return to boiling; reduce heat. Simmer, covered, about 7 minutes or until tortellini is tender. Stir in basil. If desired, serve with Parmesan cheese.

Nutrition Facts per serving: 245 cal., 5 g total fat (2 g sat. fat), 30 mg chol., 816 mg sodium, 40 g carb., 3 g dietary fiber, 13 g protein. **Daily Values:** 49 % vit. A, 140 % vit. C, 14 % calcium, 11 % iron.

TUSCAN BEAN SOUP

Start to Finish: 20 minutes | Makes: 4 servings

3 tablespoons olive oil
1 cup packaged peeled baby carrots, coarsely chopped
⅓ cup chopped onion (1 small)
2 15-ounce cans cannellini (white kidney) beans, rinsed and drained
1 32-ounce package chicken broth or 4 cups vegetable broth
2 to 3 teaspoons dried Italian seasoning, crushed
1 5-ounce package fresh baby spinach
  Cracked black pepper
  Cracker bread (optional)

1 In a 4-quart Dutch oven heat 1 tablespoon of the olive oil over medium-high heat. Add carrots and onion; cook for 3 minutes. Add beans, broth, and Italian seasoning; bring to boiling. Slightly mash beans with a potato masher; reduce heat. Simmer, uncovered, about 8 minutes or until broth is slightly thickened, stirring occasionally.

2 Meanwhile, in a large skillet heat the remaining 2 tablespoons olive oil over medium-high heat. Add spinach; toss with tongs for 1 to 2 minutes or just until wilted. Remove skillet from heat.

3 Ladle soup mixture into 4 bowls. Divide spinach evenly among the bowls. Sprinkle each with pepper. If desired, serve with cracker bread.

Nutrition Facts per serving: 254 cal., 11 g total fat (2 g sat. fat), 0 mg chol., 919 mg sodium, 36 g carb., 12 g dietary fiber, 16 g protein. **Daily Values:** 169 % vit. A, 22 % vit. C, 11 % calcium, 21 % iron.

TUSCAN BEAN SOUP

CHILLY HAM AND CUCUMBER BISQUE

Start to Finish: 17 minutes | Makes: 4 servings

- 8 ounces cubed cooked ham
- 1 English cucumber, cut up
- 3 cups buttermilk
  Salt and ground black pepper
- 1 cup packaged shredded fresh carrot
- 1 small red sweet pepper, chopped

1 In a large nonstick skillet cook ham over medium-high heat for 4 to 5 minutes or until light brown; set aside.

2 In a blender combine cucumber and buttermilk; blend until smooth. Season to taste with salt and pepper. Divide cucumber mixture among 4 soup bowls. Divide ham, carrot, and sweet pepper evenly among the bowls.

Nutrition Facts per serving: 196 cal., 7 g total fat (3 g sat. fat), 40 mg chol., 1099 mg sodium, 18 g carb., 2 g dietary fiber, 17 g protein. **Daily Values:** 107 % vit. A, 56 % vit. C, 25 % calcium, 6 % iron.

PUMPKIN-BEAN SOUP

Start to Finish: 15 minutes | Makes: 4 servings

- 1 15-ounce can pumpkin
- 1 14-ounce can unsweetened coconut milk
- 1 15-ounce can cannellini (white kidney) beans, rinsed and drained
- 1 14-ounce can vegetable broth
- 1 teaspoon dried sage, crushed
  Salt and ground black pepper
  Cracked black pepper (optional)
  Lime wedges (optional)

1 In a medium saucepan combine pumpkin, coconut milk, beans, broth, and sage. Heat through.

2 Season to taste with salt and ground black pepper. If desired, sprinkle with cracked black pepper and drizzle with juice from lime wedges.

Nutrition Facts per serving: 285 cal., 19 g total fat (17 g sat. fat), 0 mg chol., 729 mg sodium, 28 g carb., 8 g dietary fiber, 9 g protein. **Daily Values:** 335 % vit. A, 7 % vit. C, 6 % calcium, 21 % iron.

CHILLY HAM AND CUCUMBER BISQUE

BEAN-POTATO CHOWDER

Start to Finish: 20 minutes | Makes: 4 servings

- 1 **20-ounce package refrigerated diced potatoes with onions**
- 1 **14-ounce can vegetable broth**
- ⅓ **cup all-purpose flour**
- 1 **cup shredded Swiss cheese (4 ounces)**
- 3 **cups milk**
- 1 **teaspoon dried Italian seasoning, crushed**
- 1 **15-ounce can navy beans, rinsed and drained**
  - **Salt and ground black pepper**
  - **Bottled roasted red and/or yellow sweet pepper strips (optional)**
  - **Snipped fresh flat-leaf parsley (optional)**
- 8 **slices Italian bread topped with shredded Swiss cheese and toasted (optional)**

1 In a 4-quart Dutch oven combine potatoes and broth. Cover; bring to boiling over high heat. Reduce heat. Simmer, covered, for 4 minutes.

2 In a large bowl toss together flour and the 1 cup cheese until cheese is coated. Gradually stir in milk until combined. Add milk mixture and Italian seasoning to potato mixture. Cook and stir over medium heat until thickened and bubbly. Stir in beans; cook and stir about 1 minute more or until heated through. Season to taste with salt and pepper. If desired, top with sweet pepper and parsley and serve with toasted cheese-topped bread.

Nutrition Facts per serving: 494 cal., 12 g total fat (7 g sat. fat), 40 mg chol., 1344 mg sodium, 70 g carb., 9 g dietary fiber, 25 g protein. **Daily Values:** 16 % vit. A, 27 % vit. C, 50 % calcium, 19 % iron.

CORN CHOWDER

Start to Finish: 20 minutes | Makes: 4 servings

- 1 **8-ounce tub cream cheese with chives and onions**
- 1 **14.75-ounce can cream-style corn**
- 2 **cups milk**
- 8 **ounces smoked turkey breast, chopped**
- 1 **cup frozen peas**
  - **Ground black pepper**

In medium saucepan heat cream cheese over medium heat to soften. Gradually stir in corn and milk. Add turkey and peas; heat through. Season to taste with pepper.

Nutrition Facts per serving: 397 cal., 23 g total fat (15 g sat. fat), 88 mg chol., 1159 mg sodium, 27 g carb., 3 g dietary fiber, 19 g protein. **Daily Values:** 34 % vit. A, 15 % vit. C, 23 % calcium, 8 % iron.

CRAB AND CORN CHOWDER

Start to Finish: 15 minutes | Makes: 4 servings

1 14.75-ounce can cream-style corn
1 4- to 6-ounce container semi-soft cheese with garlic and herbs, cut up
1½ cups milk
1 8-ounce package flake-style imitation crabmeat
1 cup grape tomatoes, halved
2 tablespoons snipped fresh flat-leaf parsley

1 In a large saucepan combine corn and cheese; heat over low heat and stir until cheese melts. Gradually stir in milk; cook and stir until heated through.

2 Stir in crabmeat and tomatoes. Sprinkle with parsley.

Nutrition Facts per serving: 289 cal., 12 g total fat (8 g sat. fat), 45 mg chol., 816 mg sodium, 35 g carb., 2 g dietary fiber, 12 g protein. **Daily Values:** 14 % vit. A, 22 % vit. C, 14 % calcium, 5 % iron.

CREAMY TOMATO AND SHRIMP CHOWDER

Start to Finish: 18 minutes | Makes: 4 servings

1 tablespoon olive oil
1 cup chopped celery (2 stalks)
½ cup chopped onion (1 medium)
2 14.5-ounce cans diced tomatoes with basil, garlic, and oregano, undrained
8 ounces peeled, deveined cooked medium shrimp
½ cup whipping cream
½ cup water
Ground black pepper
Slivered fresh basil (optional)
Focaccia, cut into wedges (optional)

1 In a large saucepan heat olive oil over medium heat. Add celery and onion; cook just until tender.

2 Stir in undrained tomatoes; heat through. Add shrimp, whipping cream, and the water; cook over medium heat just until heated through. Season to taste with pepper. If desired, top with basil and serve with focaccia wedges.

Nutrition Facts per serving: 245 cal., 15 g total fat (8 g sat. fat), 152 mg chol., 1056 mg sodium, 14 g carb., 2 g dietary fiber, 15 g protein. **Daily Values:** 23 % vit. A, 40 % vit. C, 12 % calcium, 14 % iron.

EASY BEEF BORSCHT

Start to Finish: 18 minutes | Makes: 4 servings

1 17-ounce package refrigerated cooked beef roast au jus

1 15-ounce can julienne beets, undrained

3 cups reduced-sodium beef broth

2 cups coarsely chopped cabbage (about ⅓ of a small head)

1 medium tomato, chopped
  Ground black pepper
  Dairy sour cream (optional)

Place beef roast and juices in a large saucepan. Add undrained beets and beef broth. Bring to boiling, breaking up meat with a wooden spoon. Add cabbage and tomato. Simmer, covered, for 5 minutes. Season to taste with pepper. If desired, serve with sour cream.

Nutrition Facts per serving: 222 cal., 9 g total fat (4 g sat. fat), 64 mg chol., 1014 mg sodium, 13 g carb., 3 g dietary fiber, 26 g protein. **Daily Values:** 6 % vit. A, 31 % vit. C, 2 % calcium, 15 % iron.

PORK AND POTATO STEW

Start to Finish: 20 minutes | Makes: 4 servings

1 cup water

3 cups packaged refrigerated diced potatoes with onions

1 cup packaged julienne or shredded fresh carrot

1 teaspoon dried Italian seasoning, crushed

1 17-ounce package refrigerated cooked pork roast au jus

1 14.5-ounce can Italian-style stewed tomatoes, undrained

2 medium zucchini, halved lengthwise and cut into ½-inch slices

Salt and ground black pepper

1 In a large skillet combine the water, potatoes, carrot, and Italian seasoning. Bring to boiling; reduce heat. Simmer, covered, for 5 minutes.

2 Cut pork roast into chunks; add pork and juices from package to skillet. Stir in undrained tomatoes and zucchini. Bring to boiling; reduce heat. Simmer, covered, for 2 to 3 minutes more or until zucchini is crisp-tender. Season to taste with salt and pepper.

Nutrition Facts per serving: 296 cal., 6 g total fat (2 g sat. fat), 72 mg chol., 1123 mg sodium, 33 g carb., 6 g dietary fiber, 29 g protein. **Daily Values:** 114 % vit. A, 54 % vit. C, 5 % calcium, 14 % iron.

SAUSAGE POSOLE

Start to Finish: 20 minutes | Makes: 4 servin

1 tablespoon vegetable oil

1 pound cooked light smoked sausage, cut into 1-inch pieces

1 large sweet onion, cut into wedges

2 14.5-ounce cans Mexican-style stewed tomatoes, undrained

1 15-ounce can golden hominy, drained

1 large green sweet pepper, cut into bite-size pieces

In a Dutch oven heat oil over medium heat. Add sausage and onion; cook for 5 minutes, stirring occasionally. Drain off fat. Add undrained tomatoes, hominy, and pepper. Bring to boiling; reduce heat. Simmer, covered, for 5 minutes.

Nutrition Facts per serving: 406 cal., 20 g total fat (8 g sat. fat), 70 mg chol., 1943 mg sodium, 39 g carb., 7 g dietary fiber, 22 g protein. **Daily Values:** 5 % vit. A, 73 % vit. C, 5 % calcium, 15 % iron.

CORNBREAD-CRUSTED CHILI

Start to Finish: 20 minutes | **Makes:** 4 servings

- 1 pound ground beef
- 1 15-ounce can chili beans in chili gravy, undrained
- 1 16-ounce jar salsa
- 1 cup frozen whole kernel corn
- 1¼ cups packaged cornbread stuffing mix
- 3 tablespoons butter, melted
- 1 to 2 tablespoons snipped fresh parsley (optional)

1 Preheat broiler. In a large broiler-proof skillet cook beef until brown, stirring occasionally. Drain off fat. Stir in undrained chili beans, salsa, and corn; heat through. Spread beef mixture into an even layer.

Meanwhile, in a small bowl combine stuffing mix, butter, and, if desired, parsley. Sprinkle evenly over beef mixture. Broil 3 to 4 inches from the heat about 2 minutes or until top is golden brown.

Nutrition Facts per serving: 588 cal., 28 g total fat (12 g sat. fat), 100 mg chol., 1249 mg sodium, 53 g carb., 9 g dietary fiber, 33 g protein. **Daily Values:** 14 % vit. A, 10 % vit. C, 10 % calcium, 27 % iron.

SWEET CHILI WITH BEEF AND BEANS

Start to Finish: 20 minutes | Makes: 4 servings

1 **pound ground beef**
2 **15-ounce cans chili beans in chili sauce, undrained**
1 **16-ounce jar peach salsa**
1 **8-ounce can tomato sauce**
1 **mango, pitted, peeled, and chopped**

In a very large skillet cook beef over medium-high heat until brown. Drain off fat. Stir in undrained chili beans, salsa, and tomato sauce. Bring to boiling; reduce heat. Simmer, covered, for 10 minutes. Stir in mango just before serving.

Nutrition Facts per serving: 576 cal., 19 g total fat (7 g sat. fat), 77 mg chol., 954 mg sodium, 67 g carb., 15 g dietary fiber, 34 g protein. **Daily Values:** 65 % vit. A, 35 % vit. C, 11 % calcium, 28 % iron.

PINEAPPLE-PORK CHILI

Start to Finish: 20 minutes | Makes: 4 servings

1 **pound ground pork or beef**
1 **16-ounce jar pineapple salsa***
1 **15-ounce can red kidney beans, rinsed and drained**
1 **8-ounce can tomato sauce**
1 **tablespoon chili powder**
 Pineapple slices (optional)

In 3-quart saucepan cook meat over medium-high heat until brown. Drain off fat. Stir in salsa, beans, tomato sauce, and chili powder. Bring to boiling; reduce heat. Simmer, uncovered, for 10 minutes. If desired, serve with pineapple slices.

Nutrition Facts per serving: 356 cal., 9 g total fat (4 g sat. fat), 53 mg chol., 1026 mg sodium, 47 g carb., 5 g dietary fiber, 23 g protein. **Daily Values:** 26 % vit. A, 27 % vit. C, 6 % calcium, 23 % iron.

*TIP: If you can't locate pineapple salsa, use regular salsa and add ⅓ to ½ cup crushed pineapple.

CHAPTER 9

SALADS

CITRUS CHICKEN SALAD

Start to Finish: 13 minutes | Makes: 4 servings

3 seedless oranges

1 5- to 6-ounce package fresh baby spinach

2 6-ounce packages refrigerated grilled chicken breast strips

1 medium red sweet pepper, cut into bite-size strips

¼ cup olive oil

3 tablespoons cider vinegar

¼ teaspoon salt

⅛ teaspoon ground black pepper

⅓ cup honey-roasted-flavored sliced almonds

1 Peel and section 2 of the oranges. In a large salad bowl combine orange sections, spinach, chicken, and sweet pepper; toss to combine.

2 For dressing, finely shred 2 teaspoons peel from the remaining orange. Squeeze ¼ cup juice from the orange. In a screw-top jar place the orange juice, olive oil, vinegar, salt, and pepper. Shake to combine. Pour dressing over salad; toss to coat. Sprinkle with almonds.

Nutrition Facts per serving: 366 cal., 23 g total fat (3 g sat. fat), 55 mg chol., 961 mg sodium, 19 g carb., 5 g dietary fiber, 23 g protein. **Daily Values:** 90 % vit. A, 167 % vit. C, 11 % calcium, 13 % iron.

CHICKEN AND CABBAGE SALAD

Start to Finish: 15 minutes | Makes: 4 servings

2 tablespoons butter or margarine

1 3-ounce package ramen noodles (any flavor)

1 16-ounce package shredded cabbage with carrot (coleslaw mix)

1 7.5-ounce package frozen chopped cooked chicken, thawed

½ of a peeled, cored fresh pineapple, cut into bite-size chunks

⅔ cup bottled poppy seed or Asian toasted sesame salad dressing

1 In a large skillet melt butter over medium heat. Coarsely crumble ramen noodles; discard seasoning packet. Add noodles to skillet; cook and stir about 3 minutes or until lightly toasted. Remove from heat; set aside.

2 In a very large salad bowl combine coleslaw mix, chicken, and pineapple. Add toasted noodles; toss to combine. Pour salad dressing over salad; toss to coat.

Nutrition Facts per serving: 458 cal., 25 g total fat (9 g sat. fat), 53 mg chol., 772 mg sodium, 39 g carb., 4 g dietary fiber, 17 g protein. **Daily Values:** 47 % vit. A, 127 % vit. C, 6 % calcium, 5 % iron.

STRAWBERRY CHICKEN SALAD WITH CINNAMON PECANS

Start to Finish: 20 minutes | Makes: 4 servings

- 1 tablespoon butter or olive oil
- ½ cup pecan halves
- ¼ teaspoon ground cinnamon
- 1 5- to 6-ounce package fresh baby spinach
- 3 cups strawberries, hulled and halved
- 2 6-ounce packages refrigerated grilled chicken breast strips
- 3 medium oranges
- ¼ cup olive oil
  Salt and ground black pepper

1 In a medium skillet melt butter (or heat the 1 tablespoon olive oil) over medium heat. Add pecans and cinnamon; cook for 2 to 3 minutes or until pecans are lightly toasted. Remove from skillet; set aside.

2 On a large platter arrange spinach, half of the strawberries, and the chicken. Peel and slice 2 of the oranges and add to platter. Sprinkle with cinnamon pecans.

3 For dressing, squeeze juice from the remaining orange. In a blender combine the ¼ cup olive oil, the remaining strawberries, and the orange juice. Cover and blend until nearly smooth. Season to taste with salt and pepper. Pass dressing with salad.

Nutrition Facts per serving: 438 cal., 30 g total fat (6 g sat. fat), 63 mg chol., 965 mg sodium, 24 g carb., 7 g dietary fiber, 22 g protein. **Daily Values:** 73 % vit. A, 210 % vit. C, 10 % calcium, 15 % iron.

MEDITERRANEAN CHICKEN SALAD

Start to Finish: 20 minutes | Makes: 4 servings

8 cups packaged mixed baby greens
2 6-ounce packages refrigerated Italian or grilled chicken breast strips
1 16-ounce jar pickled mixed vegetables (giardiniera), drained
1 cup pitted kalamata olives, halved
½ cup bottled Greek salad dressing with feta cheese
½ cup onion and garlic croutons (optional)

In a very large salad bowl combine greens, chicken, mixed vegetables, and olives; toss to mix. Drizzle with dressing; toss to coat. If desired, sprinkle with croutons.

Nutrition Facts per serving: 307 cal., 21 g total fat (3 g sat. fat), 55 mg chol., 2309 mg sodium, 11 g carb., 3 g dietary fiber, 20 g protein. **Daily Values:** 80 % vit. A, 16 % vit. C, 4 % calcium, 7 % iron.

LEMONY CHICKEN AND FRUIT SALAD

Start to Finish: 20 minutes | Makes: 4 servings

6 cups packaged torn mixed salad greens
1 small cantaloupe (about 2 pounds)
2 6-ounce packages refrigerated grilled chicken breast strips
1 cup green and/or red seedless grapes
1 6-ounce carton lemon yogurt
2 tablespoons orange juice
⅛ teaspoon ground black pepper

1 Arrange greens on a platter. Halve cantaloupe; remove seeds and rind. Cut cantaloupe into chunks. Arrange cantaloupe, chicken, and grapes on top of greens.

2 For dressing, in a small bowl stir together yogurt, orange juice, and pepper. Spoon on top of salad.

Nutrition Facts per serving: 215 cal., 4 g total fat (1 g sat. fat), 58 mg chol., 824 mg sodium, 23 g carb., 2 g dietary fiber, 23 g protein. **Daily Values:** 91 % vit. A, 85 % vit. C, 11 % calcium, 8 % iron.

TURKEY-BACON SALAD

Start to Finish: 18 minutes | Makes: 4 servings

5 slices low-sodium bacon
2 cups sugar snap peas
½ cup light mayonnaise or salad dressing
1 tablespoon Dijon-style mustard
1 tablespoon cider vinegar
1 tablespoon snipped fresh dill
Salt and ground black pepper
1 small head romaine, coarsely chopped or torn
8 ounces smoked turkey breast, cut into bite-size strips

1 Line a microwave-safe 9-inch pie plate with paper towels. Arrange bacon in a single layer on top of the paper towels. Cover with additional paper towels. Cook on 100% power (high) for 4 to 5 minutes or until bacon is crisp. Carefully remove the pie plate from the microwave. Set cooked bacon slices aside to cool.

2 Meanwhile, cook the sugar snap peas, covered, in a small amount of boiling salted water for 2 to 4 minutes or until crisp-tender; drain.

3 For dressing, in a small bowl combine mayonnaise, mustard, vinegar, and dill. Season to taste with salt and pepper. Crumble 1 bacon slice; stir into dressing.

4 Divide romaine among 4 plates. Top with sugar snap peas and turkey. Break remaining bacon into 1-inch pieces; add to plates. Serve with dressing.

Nutrition Facts per serving: 258 cal., 14 g total fat (3 g sat. fat), 68 mg chol., 601 mg sodium, 9 g carb., 3 g dietary fiber, 23 g protein. **Daily Values:** 69 % vit. A, 29 % vit. C, 6 % calcium, 11 % iron.

CRANBERRY, TURKEY, AND WALNUT SALAD

Start to Finish: 15 minutes | Oven: 375°F | Makes: 4 servings

⅔ cup broken walnuts
1 8-ounce package torn mixed salad greens
1 cup grape tomatoes
8 ounces cooked turkey, thinly sliced and cut into bite-size pieces
1 cup canned whole cranberry sauce
2 tablespoons cider vinegar

1 Preheat oven to 375°F. Place walnuts in a shallow baking pan. Bake in preheated oven about 6 minutes or until toasted.

2 Meanwhile, divide greens and tomatoes among 4 plates. Top with turkey.

3 In a small bowl combine cranberry sauce and vinegar; spoon over turkey. Sprinkle with walnuts.

Nutrition Facts per serving: 344 cal., 16 g total fat (2 g sat. fat), 43 mg chol., 87 mg sodium, 32 g carb., 4 g dietary fiber, 21 g protein. **Daily Values:** 22 % vit. A, 18 % vit. C, 7 % calcium, 12 % iron.

SPICY BEEF AND NOODLE SALAD

Start to Finish: 20 minutes | Makes: 4 servings

1 pound beef flank steak
1 tablespoon soy sauce
8 ounces rice noodles
1 medium English cucumber
1 cup packaged julienne or shredded fresh carrot
½ cup Asian sweet chili sauce
½ cup water
  Fresh cilantro leaves

1 Preheat broiler. Brush steak with soy sauce. Place steak on the unheated rack of a broiler pan. Broil 4 to 5 inches from heat for 15 to 18 minutes or to desired doneness (160°F for medium), turning once halfway through broiling. Thinly slice beef across the grain.

2 Meanwhile, cook noodles according to package directions; drain in colander. Rinse with cold water.

3 Slice cucumber crosswise in three sections. Using a vegetable peeler, cut lengthwise ribbons from sections.

4 Combine chili sauce and the water. Divide steak, noodles, cucumber, and carrot among 4 bowls. Drizzle with chili sauce mixture; top with cilantro.

Nutrition Facts per serving: 477 cal., 9 g total fat (4 g sat. fat), 40 mg chol., 839 mg sodium, 70 g carb., 3 g dietary fiber, 27 g protein. **Daily Values:** 93 % vit. A, 6 % vit. C, 6 % calcium, 18 % iron.

ASIAN-STYLE BEEF AND BROCCOLI SALAD

Start to Finish: 20 minutes | **Makes:** 4 servings

- 12 ounces beef sirloin steak
- ⅔ cup bottled ginger vinaigrette salad dressing
- 3 cups packaged broccoli florets
- 8 cups packaged torn mixed salad greens
- 1 medium red sweet pepper, cut into bite-size strips

1 Trim fat from meat. Thinly slice across the grain into bite-size strips; set aside. In a wok or very large skillet heat 2 tablespoons of the salad dressing over medium-high heat. Add broccoli; cook and stir for 3 minutes. Add meat; cook and stir for 2 to 3 minutes or until meat is slightly pink in center. Remove meat and broccoli from wok.

2 In a large bowl combine greens, sweet pepper, meat strips, and broccoli. Drizzle with remaining salad dressing; toss to coat.

Nutrition Facts per serving: 237 cal., 9 g total fat (2 g sat. fat), 60 mg chol., 468 mg sodium, 17 g carb., 4 g dietary fiber, 22 g protein. **Daily Values:** 48 % vit. A, 176 % vit. C, 8 % calcium, 21 % iron.

SPINACH SALAD WITH ANCHO CHILI PEPPER PORK CHOPS

SPINACH SALAD WITH ANCHO CHILE PEPPER PORK CHOPS

Start to Finish: 20 minutes | Makes: 4 servings

1 tablespoon ground ancho chile pepper

½ teaspoon salt

½ teaspoon ground black pepper

4 boneless pork sirloin chops, ½ inch thick (about 1½ pounds)

4 slices bacon, chopped

½ cup thinly sliced red onion

⅓ cup cider vinegar

1 tablespoon sugar

¼ teaspoon ground ancho chile pepper

1 5- to 6-ounce package fresh baby spinach

1 Preheat a very large skillet over medium-high heat until very hot. In a small bowl combine the 1 tablespoon ancho chile pepper, the salt, and black pepper. Sprinkle pepper mixture on pork chops; rub mixture into the meat with your fingers. Add chops and bacon to hot skillet. Reduce heat to medium. Cook for 6 to 8 minutes or just until pork is pink in the center (160°F) and bacon is crisp, turning chops and stirring bacon occasionally. Remove and set aside.

2 For dressing, cook onion in drippings in skillet over medium heat for 1 minute. Remove skillet from heat. Stir in vinegar, sugar, and the ¼ teaspoon ancho chile pepper. Slice pork; divide pork and spinach among 4 plates. Drizzle with dressing; sprinkle with bacon.

Nutrition Facts per serving: 429 cal., 25 g total fat (8 g sat. fat), 133 mg chol., 745 mg sodium, 8 g carb., 2 g dietary fiber, 42 g protein. **Daily Values:** 80 % vit. A, 23 % vit. C, 7 % calcium, 17 % iron.

BACON AND BRIE SALAD

Start to Finish: 15 minutes | Makes: 4 servings

1 8-ounce round Brie cheese, rind removed, if desired

8 slices packaged ready-to-serve cooked bacon

1 5-ounce package spring mix salad greens

2 ripe medium pears, cored and sliced

½ cup bottled raspberry or balsamic vinaigrette salad dressing

Coarsely chopped honey-roasted cashews (optional)

1 Cut Brie cheese into 8 wedges. Wrap each wedge with a slice of bacon. Place in a microwave-safe 9-inch pie plate. Microwave, uncovered, on 50% power (medium) about 2 minutes or until cheese is slightly softened and bacon is heated through.

2 Meanwhile, divide greens among 4 plates. Fan pear slices on top of greens. Top each with 2 wedges of cheese. Drizzle with salad dressing. If desired, sprinkle with cashews.

Nutrition Facts per serving: 381 cal., 29 g total fat (13 g sat. fat), 67 mg chol., 893 mg sodium, 17 g carb., 3 g dietary fiber, 15 g protein. **Daily Values:** 16 % vit. A, 11 % vit. C, 13 % calcium, 4 % iron.

SWEET-AND-SOUR HAM SALAD

Start to Finish: 20 minutes | Makes: 4 servings

8 cups packaged torn mixed salad greens

12 ounces cubed cooked ham

2 cups fresh pea pods, halved crosswise

2 oranges, peeled and sectioned

⅓ cup mayonnaise or salad dressing

¼ cup bottled sweet-and-sour sauce

Freshly ground black pepper

¼ cup honey-roasted peanuts (optional)

Divide greens among 4 plates. Top with ham, pea pods, and orange sections. In a small bowl stir together mayonnaise and sweet-and-sour sauce; drizzle over salad. Sprinkle with freshly ground pepper. If desired, top with peanuts.

Nutrition Facts per serving: 301 cal., 18 g total fat (4 g sat. fat), 44 mg chol., 1563 mg sodium, 18 g carb., 4 g dietary fiber, 20 g protein. **Daily Values:** 30 % vit. A, 103 % vit. C, 8 % calcium, 7 % iron.

HERBED LAMB STEAK SALAD

Start to Finish: 20 minutes | Makes: 4 servings

1 pound lamb arm steaks, ½ inch thick

1 tablespoon olive oil

Salt and ground black pepper

1 5-ounce package mixed salad greens with herbs

⅔ cup sliced fresh radishes

1 6-ounce carton plain yogurt

1 to 2 tablespoons snipped fresh mint

Crumbled herbed feta cheese (optional)

1 Heat a grill pan over medium-high heat. Brush steaks with olive oil. Sprinkle lightly with salt and pepper. Cook steaks for 8 to 12 minutes or until desired doneness (160°F for medium), turning once halfway through cooking. Transfer steaks to cutting board; cover and let rest for 2 minutes.

2 Meanwhile, divide greens and radishes among 4 plates. For dressing, in a small bowl combine yogurt and mint. Season to taste with salt and pepper.

3 Remove bones from steaks; cut meat into strips. Place meat on greens. Sprinkle with cheese; pass dressing.

Nutrition Facts per serving: 344 cal., 26 g total fat (10 g sat. fat), 82 mg chol., 258 mg sodium, 5 g carb., 1 g dietary fiber, 22 g protein. **Daily Values:** 10 % vit. A, 11 % vit. C, 12 % calcium, 13 % iron.

HERBED LAMB STEAK SALAD

TUNA AND FENNEL SALAD

Start to Finish: 15 minutes | Makes: 4 servings

- 1 5- to 6-ounce package fresh baby spinach
- 2 5-ounce pouches herb and garlic–marinated chunk light tuna
- ½ of a red onion, very thinly sliced
- 1 small head fennel
- ½ cup orange juice
- ⅓ cup olive oil
- ½ teaspoon fennel seeds, crushed
- ¼ teaspoon salt
- ¼ teaspoon ground black pepper

1 Divide spinach, tuna, and onion among 4 plates. Snip enough fennel fronds to make 2 tablespoons; set aside. Very thinly slice fennel; add to salads on plates.

2 For dressing, in a screw-top jar combine orange juice, olive oil, fennel seeds, salt, pepper, and the reserved fennel fronds. Cover and shake well. Drizzle dressing over salads.

Nutrition Facts per serving: 306 cal., 22 g total fat (3 g sat. fat), 31 mg chol., 586 mg sodium, 10 g carb., 3 g dietary fiber, 18 g protein. **Daily Values:** 68 % vit. A, 48 % vit. C, 6 % calcium, 9 % iron.

FAST NIÇOISE SALAD

Start to Finish: 20 minutes | Makes: 4 servings

- 1 tablespoon butter or margarine
- 2 cups refrigerated packaged red potato wedges
- 6 cups packaged mixed salad greens
- 2 5-ounce pouches lemon-pepper chunk light tuna*
- 1 cup cherry tomatoes, halved
- ⅓ to ½ cup bottled roasted garlic vinaigrette salad dressing
  Salt and ground black pepper

1 In a large skillet melt butter over medium heat. Add potato wedges; cover and cook about 15 minutes or until golden, stirring occasionally.

2 Meanwhile, divide greens among 4 plates. Top with tuna, tomatoes, and potato wedges. Drizzle with salad dressing. Season to taste with salt and pepper.

Nutrition Facts per serving: 269 cal., 11 g total fat (1 g sat. fat), 31 mg chol., 426 mg sodium, 15 g carb., 4 g dietary fiber, 26 g protein. **Daily Values:** 16 % vit. A, 17 % vit. C, 2 % calcium, 5 % iron.

*TIP: If you can't find lemon-pepper tuna, use any herb-seasoned tuna.

SHRIMP AND ASPARAGUS SALAD

Start to Finish: 15 minutes | Makes: 4 servings

12 ounces thin asparagus spears, trimmed

6 cups watercress, tough stems removed

1 16-ounce package frozen peeled, deveined cooked shrimp with tails, thawed

2 cups cherry tomatoes, halved

¾ cup bottled light raspberry or berry vinaigrette salad dressing

Sea salt and cracked black pepper

Cracker bread (optional)

1 In a large skillet cook asparagus, covered, in a small amount of boiling lightly salted water about 3 minutes or until crisp-tender; drain in a colander. Run under cold water until cool.

2 Divide asparagus among 4 plates; top with watercress, shrimp, and tomatoes. Drizzle with dressing. Sprinkle with sea salt and cracked black pepper. If desired, serve with cracker bread.

Nutrition Facts per serving: 257 cal., 8 g total fat (1 g sat. fat), 227 mg chol., 360 mg sodium, 14 g carb., 2 g dietary fiber, 33 g protein. **Daily Values:** 58 % vit. A, 51 % vit. C, 14 % calcium, 25 % iron.

CRAB ON SWEET PEPPERS

Start to Finish: 12 minutes | Makes: 4 servings

2 large red, green, and/or yellow sweet peppers, cut into bite-size strips

1 8-ounce package chunk-style imitation crabmeat

2 medium tomatoes, coarsely chopped

1 English cucumber, halved and thinly sliced

½ cup bottled reduced-calorie Thousand Island salad dressing

Arrange sweet pepper strips on a serving platter. Top with crabmeat, tomatoes, and cucumber. Drizzle with salad dressing.

Nutrition Facts per serving: 156 cal., 5 g total fat (0 g sat. fat), 12 mg chol., 733 mg sodium, 24 g carb., 3 g dietary fiber, 6 g protein. **Daily Values:** 51 % vit. A, 143 % vit. C, 3 % calcium, 6 % iron.

CHAPTER 10

DESSERTS

MOCHA POUND CAKE

Start to Finish: 20 minutes | Makes: 4 servings

½ of a 10.75-ounce frozen pound cake, thawed
3 tablespoons sugar
2 tablespoons unsweetened cocoa powder
1 teaspoon instant coffee crystals
⅓ cup milk
1 3-ounce package cream cheese, softened
1 medium orange
Orange slices, cut into eighths, or orange peel curls (optional)

1 Preheat broiler. Cut pound cake into 8 thin slices; place on a baking sheet. Broil, 3 to 4 inches from heat, for 1 to 2 minutes per side or until toasted. In a small bowl whisk together sugar, cocoa powder, and coffee crystals. Gradually whisk in milk until smooth.

2 In a medium mixing bowl beat cream cheese with an electric mixer on medium speed until smooth. Gradually beat in the milk mixture until smooth, scraping sides of bowl as needed.

3 Peel orange and cut crosswise into 4 slices. Place a pound cake slice on each of 4 dessert plates. Add an orange slice and the cream cheese mixture to each. Top with remaining pound cake slices. If desired, garnish with additional orange slice pieces.

Nutrition Facts per serving: 291 cal., 16 g total fat (10 g sat. fat), 109 mg chol., 224 mg sodium, 35 g carb., 2 g dietary fiber, 5 g protein. **Daily Values:** 13 % vit. A, 29 % vit. C, 7 % calcium, 7 % iron.

RASPBERRY-LEMON CAKE

Start to Finish: 15 minutes | Makes: 4 servings

½ cup whipping cream
1 tablespoon sugar
¼ cup lemon curd
4 slices purchased angel food cake (about ¼ of an 8- to 9-inch cake)
2 cups fresh raspberries
Thin strips lemon peel (optional)

1 In a chilled medium mixing bowl beat whipping cream and sugar with an electric mixer on medium speed until soft peaks form. Stir lemon curd to soften. Beat lemon curd into whipped cream just until stiff peaks form.

2 Place a cake slice on each of 4 dessert plates. Top with the whipped cream mixture and raspberries. If desired, garnish with lemon peel strips.

Nutrition Facts per serving: 341 cal., 13 g total fat (7 g sat. fat), 56 mg chol., 282 mg sodium, 56 g carb., 6 g dietary fiber, 4 g protein. **Daily Values:** 9 % vit. A, 27 % vit. C, 8 % calcium, 3 % iron.

QUICK STRAWBERRY CHEESECAKE

Start to Finish: 20 minutes | **Makes:** 4 servings

- **2 ounces Brie cheese, softened**
- **1 3-ounce package cream cheese, softened**
- **2 to 3 tablespoons sugar**
- **1 teaspoon lemon juice**
- **2 cups fresh strawberries, hulled and sliced**
- **½ cup butter toffee–glazed sliced almonds**
- **Honey (optional)**

1 Remove and discard the rind from the Brie cheese. In a medium mixing bowl beat Brie, cream cheese, sugar, and lemon juice with an electric mixer on medium speed until almost smooth; set aside.

2 Divide strawberries, cheese mixture, and almonds among 4 parfait glasses or water goblets, alternating layers of berries, cheese, and almonds. If desired, drizzle with honey.

Nutrition Facts per serving: 249 cal., 18 g total fat (7 g sat. fat), 38 mg chol., 213 mg sodium, 17 g carb., 3 g dietary fiber, 7 g protein. **Daily Values:** 8 % vit. A, 72 % vit. C, 9 % calcium, 3 % iron.

NUTTY MAPLE PUDDING

Start to Finish: 20 minutes | Oven: 350°F | Makes: 4 servings

- ½ cup pecan pieces
- ½ cup whipping cream
- 1 4-serving-size package vanilla or white chocolate instant pudding and pie filling mix
- 2 cups milk
- 3 tablespoons pure maple syrup (optional)
- 1 medium pear, cored and thinly sliced
- ⅓ cup pure maple syrup

1 Preheat oven to 350°F. Spread pecan pieces in a shallow baking pan. Bake for 5 to 10 minutes or until toasted.

2 Meanwhile, in a chilled medium mixing bowl beat whipping cream with an electric mixer on medium speed until soft peaks form; set aside. Prepare pudding mix according to package directions, using the 2 cups milk. If desired, stir in the 3 tablespoons maple syrup. Fold whipped cream into pudding mixture.

3 Divide pudding mixture among 4 dessert dishes. Top with pear slices. In a small bowl combine the toasted pecans and the 1/3 cup maple syrup. Spoon pecan mixture over pudding and pear slices.

Nutrition Facts per serving: 447 cal., 24 g total fat (9 g sat. fat), 51 mg chol., 424 mg sodium, 56 g carb., 3 g dietary fiber, 6 g protein. **Daily Values:** 14 % vit. A, 4 % vit. C, 20 % calcium, 4 % iron.

QUICK CHERRY CRISP

Start to Finish: 20 minutes | **Makes:** 4 servings

⅓ to ½ cup sugar
1 tablespoon cornstarch
4 cups frozen unsweetened pitted tart red cherries
1 cup crumbled shortbread cookies
2 tablespoons butter or margarine, melted
¼ cup pecans or almonds, toasted and chopped
Ice cream (optional)

1 In a small bowl combine sugar and cornstarch. Place cherries in a large saucepan; sprinkle cornstarch mixture over cherries; stir to combine. Cook over medium heat about 10 minutes or until thickened and bubbly; cook and stir for 2 minutes more.

2 Meanwhile, in a medium bowl thoroughly combine crumbled cookies, butter, and nuts.

3 Divide cherry mixture among 4 dessert dishes. Sprinkle cookie mixture over cherry mixture. If desired, serve with ice cream.

Nutrition Facts per serving: 362 cal., 17 g total fat (6 g sat. fat), 20 mg chol., 152 mg sodium, 52 g carb., 4 g dietary fiber, 4 g protein. **Daily Values:** 31 % vit. A, 5 % vit. C, 4 % calcium, 9 % iron.

STOVETOP PEACH-RASPBERRY COBBLER

Start to Finish: 20 minutes | **Oven:** 375°F | **Makes:** 4 servings

1 teaspoon sugar
Dash ground cinnamon
½ of a sheet frozen puff pastry, thawed according to package directions
1 egg, lightly beaten
3 tablespoons sugar
1 tablespoon cornstarch
¼ teaspoon ground cinnamon
1 16-ounce package frozen unsweetened peach slices
1 cup fresh raspberries
½ cup water
Vanilla ice cream (optional)

1 For puff pastry twists, preheat oven to 375°F. In a small bowl combine the 1 teaspoon sugar and the dash cinnamon. Place puff pastry on work surface. Brush pastry with beaten egg. Sprinkle with cinnamon-sugar mixture. Cut pastry lengthwise into 4 strips; cut each strip in half crosswise. Twist strips; place on a greased baking sheet. Bake about 15 minutes or until brown and puffed.

2 Meanwhile, in a large saucepan combine the 3 tablespoons sugar, the cornstarch, and the ¼ teaspoon cinnamon. Add frozen peaches, half of the raspberries, and the water. Cook over medium heat until mixture is thickened and bubbly. Cook and stir for 2 minutes more. Remove from heat. Stir in the remaining raspberries.

3 Top fruit mixture with puff pastry twists. If desired, serve with ice cream.

Nutrition Facts per serving: 159 cal., 4 g total fat (1 g sat. fat), 53 mg chol., 34 mg sodium, 30 g carb., 4 g dietary fiber, 3 g protein. **Daily Values:** 9 % vit. A, 26 % vit. C, 2 % calcium, 5 % iron.

TIP: Cut 1 sheet puff pastry into 16 strips (about 1⅛x4½ inch); brush with the egg and sprinkle with mixture of 2 teaspoons sugar and ⅛ teaspoon ground cinnamon. Twist and bake as above. Serve half the strips with cobbler. Cool remaining strips; place in airtight freezer container and freeze up to 2 months for the next time you want the cobbler.

BRIE APPLE QUESADILLAS

Start to Finish: 20 minutes | Oven: 400°F | Makes: 4 quesadillas

4 7- to 8-inch flour tortillas
1 tablespoon butter or margarine, melted
4 ounces Brie cheese, cut into 1/4-inch slices (remove rind, if desired) or 1 cup shredded cheddar cheese
2 large cooking apples (such as Granny Smith), peeled, cored, and very thinly sliced
1/2 cup chopped walnuts
2 tablespoons packed brown sugar
2 to 3 tablespoons caramel-flavored ice cream topping

1 Preheat oven to 400°F. Brush one side of each tortilla with melted butter. Place tortillas, buttered sides down, on a large baking sheet. Place Brie cheese on one half of each tortilla. Arrange apples and walnuts on top of cheese. Sprinkle with brown sugar. Fold other half of each tortilla over apple-nut mixture.

2 Bake for 8 to 10 minutes or until golden brown and cheese melts. Transfer quesadillas to a serving platter or 4 dessert plates. Drizzle caramel topping over quesadillas.

Nutrition Facts per quesadilla: 462 cal., 23 g total fat (8 g sat. fat), 36 mg chol., 487 mg sodium, 54 g carb., 3 g dietary fiber, 13 g protein. **Dzaily Values:** 6 % vit. A, 7 % vit. C, 18 % calcium, 10 % iron.

WONTON DESSERT STACKS

Start to Finish: 20 minutes | Oven: 350°F | Makes: 4 servings

Nonstick cooking spray
8 wonton wrappers
Sugar
½ cup sliced strawberries
2 kiwi fruit, peeled and sliced
1 6-ounce carton low-fat lemon yogurt
2 fresh strawberries, cut in half

1 Preheat oven to 350°F. Line a large baking sheet with foil; lightly coat with cooking spray. Place wontons flat on the baking sheet; lightly coat with additional cooking spray. Sprinkle lightly with sugar. Bake for 6 to 8 minutes or until golden brown and crisp. Remove from oven; cool slightly.

2 Meanwhile, in a medium bowl combine the ½ cup sliced strawberries and kiwi fruit.

3 To assemble, place 1 baked wonton wrapper on each of 4 dessert plates. Top each with some of the yogurt. Divide the fruit mixture evenly among the stacks. Add another baked wonton. Top with remaining yogurt. Garnish each stack with a strawberry half.

Nutrition Facts per serving: 127 cal., 1 g total fat (0 g sat. fat), 4 mg chol., 118 mg sodium, 26 g carb., 2 g dietary fiber, 4 g protein. **Daily Values:** 1 % vit. A, 83 % vit. C, 9 % calcium, 4 % iron.

CREAMY PARFAITS

Start to Finish: 20 minutes | Makes: 4 servings

1 4-serving-size package French vanilla instant pudding and pie filling mix
1 cup milk
½ cup mascarpone or cream cheese, softened
¼ cup whipping cream
1 cup crushed biscotti or shortbread cookies (5 biscotti or 16 shortbread cookies)
1 cup fresh berries (such as blueberries, raspberries, and/or hulled, sliced strawberries)

1 Prepare pudding mix according to package directions using the 1 cup milk. Stir cheese until smooth. Gradually stir ½ cup of the pudding into cheese. Fold pudding-cheese mixture back into the remaining pudding.

2 In a chilled small bowl beat whipping cream with an electric mixer on medium speed until soft peaks form. Fold whipped cream into pudding mixture; set aside.

3 To assemble parfaits, divide half of the crushed biscotti among 4 parfait glasses or water goblets. Divide half of the berries and pudding mixture among the glasses to create layers. Repeat with remaining crushed biscotti, berries, and pudding. Serve immediately or cover and chill up to 4 hours.

Nutrition Facts per serving: 492 cal., 25 g total fat (14 g sat. fat), 74 mg chol., 510 mg sodium, 61 g carb., 2 g dietary fiber, 12 g protein. **Daily Values:** 7 % vit. A, 6 % vit. C, 8 % calcium, 4 % iron.

INDIVIDUAL BROWNIE TRIFLES

Start to Finish: 20 minutes | Makes: 4 servings

- ⅔ cup whipping cream
- 1 tablespoon sugar
- ¼ teaspoon vanilla
- 8 2x2-inch purchased baked brownies, crumbled into pieces (about 2 cups)
- 2 cups fresh raspberries or dark sweet cherries, pitted
- 1 cup chocolate ice cream topping
  Unsweetened cocoa powder (optional)

1 In a chilled large mixing bowl beat whipping cream, sugar, and vanilla with an electric mixer on medium speed until soft peaks form; set aside.

2 Divide half of the crumbled brownies among 4 large parfait glasses or water goblets. Divide half of the raspberries, ice cream topping, and whipped cream among the glasses, creating layers. Repeat layers with remaining brownies, raspberries, ice cream topping, and whipped cream. If desired, sprinkle with cocoa powder. Serve immediately or cover and chill up to 4 hours.

Nutrition Facts per serving: 627 cal., 29 g total fat (13 g sat. fat), 90 mg chol., 240 mg sodium, 88 g carb., 7 g dietary fiber, 9 g protein. **Daily Values:** 20 % vit. A, 27 % vit. C, 11 % calcium, 11 % iron.

PB&J ICE CREAM SUNDAES

Start to Finish: 15 minutes | Makes: 4 servings

- ¼ cup raspberry, strawberry, or grape jelly or jam
- 1 cup chopped strawberries, sliced peaches, blueberries, and/or quartered grapes
- 1 pint vanilla or chocolate ice cream
- 4 soft bakery peanut butter cookies, broken
- ¼ cup honey-roasted peanuts, chopped

1 In a small saucepan heat jelly over low heat just until smooth. Stir in fruit.

2 Scoop ice cream into each of 4 dessert dishes or bowls. Top ice cream with fruit mixture. Add broken cookies to each. Sprinkle with peanuts.

Nutrition Facts per serving: 472 cal., 26 g total fat (13 g sat. fat), 106 mg chol., 179 mg sodium, 56 g carb., 2 g dietary fiber, 7 g protein. **Daily Values:** 14 % vit. A, 36 % vit. C, 14 % calcium, 7 % iron.

CHOCOLATE-RICOTTA PHYLLO SHELLS

Start to Finish: 20 minutes | Makes: 15 miniature tarts

- ¾ cup ricotta cheese
- 1 tablespoon sugar
- 1 teaspoon unsweetened cocoa powder
- ¼ teaspoon vanilla
- 3 tablespoons miniature semisweet chocolate pieces
- 1 2.1-ounce package baked miniature phyllo shells (15)

1 For filling, in a medium bowl combine cheese, sugar, cocoa powder, and vanilla. Stir until smooth. Fold in 2 tablespoons of the chocolate pieces.

2 Using two spoons, scoop the filling into phyllo shells. Top with remaining chocolate pieces. Serve immediately or cover and chill up to 2 hours.

Nutrition Facts per tart: 62 cal., 3 g total fat (1 g sat. fat), 6 mg chol., 20 mg sodium, 6 g carb., 0 g dietary fiber, 2 g protein. **Daily Values:** 1 % vit. A, 0 % vit. C, 3 % calcium, 2 % iron.

BANANAS SUZETTE

Start to Finish: 15 minutes | Makes: 4 servings

- 2 ripe, yet firm, medium bananas
- ¼ cup orange juice
- 3 tablespoons sugar
- 1 tablespoon butter or margarine
- ¼ cup dried tart cherries
- ⅛ teaspoon ground nutmeg
- 2 cups vanilla ice cream

1 Peel bananas; bias-slice each banana into 8 pieces. In a large skillet combine orange juice, sugar, and butter; heat about 1 minute or until butter melts and sugar dissolves. Add the bananas and cherries; heat for 2 to 4 minutes more or just until bananas are tender, stirring once. Stir in nutmeg.

2 To serve, divide vanilla ice cream among 4 dessert bowls. Spoon bananas and sauce over ice cream.

Nutrition Facts per serving: 302 cal., 11 g total fat (7 g sat. fat), 39 mg chol., 83 mg sodium, 51 g carb., 3 g dietary fiber, 3 g protein. **Daily Values:** 12 % vit. A, 22 % vit. C, 11 % calcium, 2 % iron.

PEACHES WITH RICOTTA FLUFF

Start to Finish: 15 minutes | Makes: 4 servings

- 1 cup ricotta cheese
- ½ cup milk
- 1 4-serving-size package white chocolate instant pudding and pie filling mix
- ¼ cup macadamia nuts, chopped
- 3 peaches, pitted and sliced

1 In a food processor combine cheese and milk; cover and process until smooth. Add pudding mix; cover and process until mixture thickens. Fold in half of the macadamia nuts.

2 Divide ricotta mixture among 4 dessert dishes. Top with peach slices. Sprinkle with remaining macadamia nuts.

Nutrition Facts per serving: 316 cal., 15 g total fat (7 g sat. fat), 34 mg chol., 436 mg sodium, 38 g carb., 2 g dietary fiber, 10 g protein. **Daily Values:** 14 % vit. A, 13 % vit. C, 18 % calcium, 4 % iron.

WARM SPICED PEACHES

Start to Finish: 15 minutes | Makes: 4 servings

3 ripe medium peaches, peeled and sliced
1 tablespoon sugar
½ teaspoon ground cinnamon
½ teaspoon finely shredded orange peel
½ teaspoon vanilla
¼ teaspoon ground nutmeg
1 6-ounce carton vanilla yogurt

1 In a medium bowl combine peaches, sugar, cinnamon, orange peel, vanilla, and nutmeg; toss gently to combine. Divide among four 5-inch individual quiche dishes or 10-ounce custard cups.

2 Place dishes, 2 at a time, in a microwave oven. Microwave on 100% power (high) for 1 to 1½ minutes or until warm. Serve with yogurt.

Nutrition Facts per serving: 95 cal., 1 g total fat (0 g sat. fat), 2 mg chol., 28 mg sodium, 20 g carb., 2 g dietary fiber, 3 g protein. **Daily Values:** 8 % vit. A, 14 % vit. C, 8 % calcium, 2 % iron.

CARAMELIZED APPLES WITH ICE CREAM

Start to Finish: 20 minutes | Makes: 4 servings

⅓ cup sugar
1 teaspoon ground cinnamon
1 tablespoon butter
4 firm cooking apples (such as Braeburn or Jonagold), halved lengthwise and cored
½ cup water
2 cups vanilla ice cream
Cinnamon sugar (optional)

1 On a plate combine sugar and cinnamon. Heat a very large skillet over medium heat. Add butter. Press the cut side of each apple into the cinnamon-sugar mixture. Place apples, cut sides down, in the hot skillet. Sprinkle with any remaining cinnamon-sugar mixture.

2 Cook apples for 7 to 8 minutes or just until apples begin to brown. Add the ½ cup water; cover and reduce heat to low. Simmer for 5 to 7 minutes, adding more water if sugar begins to burn.

3 Remove apples from skillet. Place 2 apple halves on each of 4 plates; drizzle with sauce from skillet. Add a scoop of ice cream to each plate. If desired, sprinkle with cinnamon sugar.

Nutrition Facts per serving: 304 cal., 11 g total fat (7 g sat. fat), 33 mg chol., 58 mg sodium, 51 g carb., 4 g dietary fiber, 2 g protein. **Daily Values:** 11 % vit. A, 11 % vit. C, 8 % calcium, 1 % iron.

HONEY-MELONS WITH SHERBET

Start to Finish: 20 minutes | Makes: 4 servings

- 4 cups purchased cubed melon
- 1 medium banana, peeled and sliced (¾ cup)
- 2 tablespoons honey
- 1 tablespoon orange juice
- 1 tablespoon snipped fresh mint (optional)
- 2 cups orange sherbet or sorbet

1 In a medium bowl combine melon and banana. Drizzle honey and orange juice over fruit; gently toss to mix. If desired, stir in mint.

2 Spoon melon mixture into 4 dessert bowls. Top each with a scoop of orange sherbet.

Nutrition Facts per serving: 216 cal., 2 g total fat (1 g sat. fat), 1 mg chol., 48 mg sodium, 51 g carb., 3 g dietary fiber, 2 g protein. **Daily Values:** 64 % vit. A, 70 % vit. C, 6 % calcium, 3 % iron.

DOUBLE BERRY SOUP

Start to Finish: 20 minutes | Makes: 4 servings

- 2 cup sliced strawberries
- 2 cups blueberries
- ¾ cup orange juice
- ¼ cup sugar
- 2 cups lemon or other citrus sorbet
  Fresh mint leaves (optional)

1 In a medium saucepan combine strawberries, blueberries, orange juice, and sugar; cook over medium heat for 4 to 5 minutes or just until bubbly, stirring occasionally. Remove from heat. Let stand about 5 minutes to slightly cool the mixture.

2 Ladle the soup into 4 shallow dessert bowls. Top each with a scoop of sorbet. If desired, garnish with fresh mint.

Nutrition Facts per serving: 244 cal., 1 g total fat (0 g sat. fat), 0 mg chol., 27 mg sodium, 61 g carb., 4 g dietary fiber, 1 g protein. **Daily Values:** 3 % vit. A, 125 % vit. C, 4 % calcium, 3 % iron.

DOUBLE BERRY SOUP

HOT FUDGE SAUCE

Start to Finish: 15 minutes | **Makes:** 1¼ cups sauce

⅓ cup unsweetened cocoa powder

½ cup granulated sugar

⅓ cup packed brown sugar

3 tablespoons butter or margarine

½ cup whipping cream

1 In a small bowl stir together cocoa powder, granulated sugar, and brown sugar; set aside.

2 In a small heavy saucepan heat butter and whipping cream over low heat until butter melts, stirring constantly. Cook and stir over medium heat about 3 minutes more or until mixture bubbles around edges. Add cocoa mixture; cook, stirring constantly, for 1 to 2 minutes more or until sugar is dissolved and mixture is smooth and slightly thickened.

3 Serve warm sauce (sauce will continue to thicken when cooling) over fruit, ice cream, cake, cheesecake, or pastry desserts.

Nutrition Facts per 2 tablespoons sauce: 145 cal., 8 g total fat (5 g sat. fat), 26 mg chol., 32 mg sodium, 19 g carb., 1 g dietary fiber, 1 g protein. **Daily Values:** 6 % vit. A, 0 % vit. C, 2 % calcium, 2 % iron.

TIP: Store sauce in the refrigerator for up to 1 week. To reheat on stovetop, in a small heavy saucepan heat and stir sauce over low heat, stirring frequently. To reheat in microwave, place chilled topping in a 2-cup glass measuring cup. Microwave, uncovered, on 100% power (high) for 1 to 2 minutes or until heated through, stirring twice.

RASPBERRY SAUCE

Start to Finish: 20 minutes | **Makes:** 1¼ cups sauce

2 cups fresh or frozen raspberries

3 tablespoons sugar

½ teaspoon cornstarch

1 Thaw raspberries, if frozen. Do not drain. Place 1½ cups of the raspberries in a food processor or blender; cover and process or blend until smooth. Press raspberries through a fine-mesh sieve; discard seeds.

2 In a small saucepan stir together sugar and cornstarch. Add raspberry puree; cook and stir over medium heat until thickened and bubbly. Cook and stir for 2 minutes more. Transfer to a small bowl. Serve warm or chilled. Stir in the remaining ½ cup whole raspberries before serving. Serve over angel food cake, cheesecake, or ice cream.

Nutrition Facts per 2 tablespoons sauce: 28 cal., 0 g total fat (0 g sat. fat), 0 mg chol., 0 mg sodium, 7 g carb., 2 g dietary fiber, 0 g protein. **Daily Values:** 0 % vit. A, 11 % vit. C, 1 % calcium, 1 % iron.

TIP: Store any leftover sauce in a covered container in the refrigerator for up to 1 week. Stir sauce before serving.

CARAMEL SAUCE

Start to Finish: 10 minutes | **Makes:** ¾ cup sauce

½ cup packed brown sugar

1 tablespoon cornstarch

¼ cup water

⅓ cup half-and-half or light cream

2 tablespoons light-colored corn syrup

1 tablespoon butter or margarine

½ teaspoon vanilla

1 In a small heavy saucepan stir together brown sugar and cornstarch over medium heat. Stir in the water. Stir in half-and-half, corn syrup, and butter; cook and stir until bubbly (mixture may appear curdled). Cook and stir for 2 minutes more. Remove from heat; stir in vanilla.

2 Serve warm or cooled sauce over ice cream, fruit, cake, or cheesecake.

Nutrition Facts per 2 tablespoons sauce: 121 cal., 3 g total fat (2 g sat. fat), 10 mg chol., 27 mg sodium, 23 g carb., 0 g dietary fiber, 0 g protein. **Daily Values:** 2 % vit. A, 0 % vit. C, 3 % calcium, 1 % iron.

TIP: Store any leftover sauce in a covered container in the refrigerator for up to 3 days. To serve, let sauce stand at room temperature for 30 minutes before serving or warm sauce in a small saucepan over low heat. Stir sauce before serving.

INDEX

Note: Page numbers in *italics* refer to illustrations.

METRIC INFORMATION

The charts on this page provide a guide for converting measurements from the U.S. customary system, which is used throughout this book, to the metric system.

PRODUCT DIFFERENCES

Most of the ingredients called for in the recipes in this book are available in most countries. However, some are known by different names. Here are some common American ingredients and their possible counterparts:

- Sugar (white) is granulated, fine granulated, or castor sugar.
- Powdered sugar is icing sugar.
- All-purpose flour is enriched, bleached, or unbleached white household flour. When self-rising flour is used in place of all-purpose flour in a recipe that calls for leavening, omit the leavening agent (baking soda or baking powder) and salt.
- Light-colored corn syrup is golden syrup.
- Cornstarch is cornflour.
- Baking soda is bicarbonate of soda.
- Vanilla or vanilla extract is vanilla essence.
- Green, red, or yellow sweet peppers are capsicums or bell peppers.
- Golden raisins are sultanas.

VOLUME AND WEIGHT

The United States traditionally uses cup measures for liquid and solid ingredients. The chart, top right, shows the approximate imperial and metric equivalents. If you are accustomed to weighing solid ingredients, the following approximate equivalents will be helpful.

- 1 cup butter, castor sugar, or rice = 8 ounces = ½ pound = 250 grams
- 1 cup flour = 4 ounces = ¼ pound = 125 grams
- 1 cup icing sugar = 5 ounces = 150 grams

Canadian and U.S. volume for a cup measure is 8 fluid ounces (237 ml), but the standard metric equivalent is 250 ml.

1 British imperial cup is 10 fluid ounces.

In Australia, 1 tablespoon equals 20 ml, and there are 4 teaspoons in the Australian tablespoon.

Spoon measures are used for smaller amounts of ingredients. Although the size of the tablespoon varies slightly in different countries, for practical purposes and for recipes in this book, a straight substitution is all that's necessary. Measurements made using cups or spoons always should be level unless stated otherwise.

COMMON WEIGHT RANGE REPLACEMENTS

Imperial / U.S.	Metric
½ ounce	15 g
1 ounce	25 g or 30 g
4 ounces (¼ pound)	115 g or 125 g
8 ounces (½ pound)	225 g or 250 g
16 ounces (1 pound)	450 g or 500 g
1¼ pounds	625 g
1½ pounds	750 g
2 pounds or 2¼ pounds	1,000 g or 1 Kg

OVEN TEMPERATURE EQUIVALENTS

Fahrenheit Setting	Celsius Setting*	Gas Setting
300°F	150°C	Gas Mark 2 (very low)
325°F	160°C	Gas Mark 3 (low)
350°F	180°C	Gas Mark 4 (moderate)
375°F	190°C	Gas Mark 5 (moderate)
400°F	200°C	Gas Mark 6 (hot)
425°F	220°C	Gas Mark 7 (hot)
450°F	230°C	Gas Mark 8 (very hot)
475°F	240°C	Gas Mark 9 (very hot)
500°F	260°C	Gas Mark 10 (extremely hot)
Broil	Broil	Grill

*Electric and gas ovens may be calibrated using celsius. However, for an electric oven, increase celsius setting 10 to 20 degrees when cooking above 160°C. For convection or forced air ovens (gas or electric) lower the temperature setting 25°F/10°C when cooking at all heat levels.

BAKING PAN SIZES

Imperial / U.S.	Metric
9×1½-inch round cake pan	22- or 23×4-cm (1.5 L)
9×1½-inch pie plate	22- or 23×4-cm (1 L)
8×8×2-inch square cake pan	20×5-cm (2 L)
9×9×2-inch square cake pan	22- or 23×4.5-cm (2.5 L)
11×7×1½-inch baking pan	28×17×4-cm (2 L)
2-quart rectangular baking pan	30×19×4.5-cm (3 L)
13×9×2-inch baking pan	34×22×4.5-cm (3.5 L)
15×10×1-inch jelly roll pan	40×25×2-cm
9×5×3-inch loaf pan	23×13×8-cm (2 L)
2-quart casserole	2 L

U.S. / STANDARD METRIC EQUIVALENTS

⅛ teaspoon = 0.5 ml	⅓ cup = 3 fluid ounces = 75 ml
¼ teaspoon = 1 ml	½ cup = 4 fluid ounces = 125 ml
½ teaspoon = 2 ml	⅔ cup = 5 fluid ounces = 150 ml
1 teaspoon = 5 ml	¾ cup = 6 fluid ounces = 175 ml
1 tablespoon = 15 ml	1 cup = 8 fluid ounces = 250 ml
2 tablespoons = 25 ml	2 cups = 1 pint = 500 ml
¼ cup = 2 fluid ounces = 50 ml	1 quart = 1 litre